CORIOLANO CIPPICO

THE DEEDS OF COMMANDER PIETRO MOCENIGO

CORIOLANO CIPPICO

THE DEEDS OF COMMANDER PIETRO MOCENIGO IN THREE BOOKS

INTRODUCTION,
TRANSLATION
AND NOTES
BY
KIRIL PETKOV

ITALICA PRESS
NEW YORK
2014

Copyright © 2014 by Kiril Petkov

ITALICA PRESS, INC.
595 Main Street
New York, New York 10044
inquiries@italicapress.com

Italica Press Medieval & Renaissance Texts

All rights reserved. No part of this publication may be reproduced, stored in a retrieval system, or transmitted, in any form or by any means, electronic, mechanical, photocopying, recording or otherwise, without prior permission of Italica Press. For permission to reproduce selected portions for courses, please contact the Press at inquiries@italicapress.com.

Library of Congress Cataloging-in-Publication Data

Cippico, Coriolano, 1425?–1493?

[De Petri Mocenici imperatoris gestis libri tres. English]

Coriolano Cippico : the deeds of Commander Pietro Mocenigo in three books : introduction, translation, and notes / by Kiril Petkov.
  pages cm. -- (Medieval & renaissance texts)

Includes bibliographical references and index.

ISBN 978-1-59910-295-5 (hardcover : alk. paper) -- ISBN 978-1-59910-296-2 (pbk. : alk. paper) -- ISBN 978-1-59910-297-9 (e-book)

1. Venice (Italy)--History--Turkish Wars, 1453-1571. 2. Turkey--History--1288-1453. 3. Austria--History--1273-1519. 4. Sigmund, Archduke of Austria, 1427-1496. I. Petkov, Kiril, 1964-, translator. II. Title. III. Title: Deeds of Commander Pietro Mocenigo in three books, introduction, translation, and notes.

DG678.2.C5613 2014

956 .015--dc23

[B]

2014032554

Cover art: Durazzo. From Simon Pinargenti, *Isole che son da Venetia nella Dalmatia....* Venice: Simon Pinargenti et Compani, 1573.

FOR A COMPLETE LIST OF ITALICA PRESS TITLES
VISIT OUR WEB SITE AT:
WWW.ITALICAPRESS.COM

CONTENTS

List of Illustrations	VI
Maps	VII
Acknowledgments	VIII
Introduction: Coriolano Cippico, His Work and His Times	XIII
The Author	XIII
Subject Matter	XIX
Form and Themes	XXIV
This Edition	XXXV
The Deeds of Commander Pietro Mocenigo in Three Books	1
Dedication	1
Book One	3
Book Two	35
Book Three	63
Bibliography	93
Early Modern Editions of the Latin Text	93
Modern Editions and Translations	93
Other Primary Sources	93
Secondary Works	94
Index	101

✶

ILLUSTRATIONS

Frontispiece. Portrait of Pietro Mocenigo by Gentile Bellini.
Bologna, Fondazione Federico Zeri. II
Fig. 1 Pietro Lombardo., Portrait statue of Pietro Mocenigo.
Funerary Monument of Doge Pietro Mocenigo. SS. Giovanni e
Paolo, Venice. XII
Fig. 2. Palazzo Cippico, Trogir. Birthplace of Coriolano Cippico.
Author XV
Fig. 3. The Quai of Cippico's Castel Vecchio. From F. Hamilton
Jackson, *The Shores of the Adriatic: The Austrian Side.*
London: John Murray, 1908. XIX
Fig. 4. Pietro Lombardo. Funerary Monument of Doge
Pietro Mocenigo. SS. Giovanni e Paolo, Venice. XXXVIII
Fig. 5. Rhodes. From Hartmann Schedel, *Nuremberg Chronicle.*
Nuremberg: Anton Koberger, 1493. 10
Fig. 6. Modon. From Bernhard von Breydenbach,
Peregrinatio in terram sanctam. Mainz: Erhard Reuwich, 1488. 12
Fig. 7. Pergamum. Theater and Palace District.
Wikimedia Commons. 14
Fig. 8. Delos, Temple of Apollo. From Victor Duruy,
History of Greece. Boston: Estes and Lauriat, 1890. 17
Fig. 9. The Tomb of Mausoleus, Halicarnassus. Engraving by
Philips Galle after Maerten van Heemskerck, *Seven Wonders
of the World,* 1572. 21
Fig. 10. Smyrna. From Mark Twain, *Innocents Abroad.* Hartford, CT:
American Publishing Co., 1869. 31
Fig. 11. Turkish Fortifications on the Dardanelles. From Giovanni
Francesco Camocio, Dardanelo fortezza dala parte dela Grecia....
From *Isole famose, porti, fortezze, e terre maritime.* Venice: Alla libraria
del segno di S. Marco, 1572. 34
Fig. 12. The Temple of Aphrodite at Aphrodisias.
From Charles Fellows, *An Account of Discoveries in Lycia.*
London: J. Murray, 1841. 41

ILLUSTRATIONS AND MAPS ✳

Fig. 13. Corycus. From Victor Langlois, *Voyage dans la Cilicie et dans les montagnes du Taurus exécuté pendant les années 1852–1853*. Paris: B. Duprat, 1861. 45

Fig. 14. Seleucia. Ruins of Tombs. Wikimedia Commons. 49

Fig. 15. Famagusta by Giovanni Francesco Camocio. From Braun and Hogenberg, *Civitates Orbis Terrarum I*. Cologne: Typis Theodori Graminaei, 1572. 62

Fig. 16. Map of Scutari by Giovanni Francesco Camocio, c. 1570. 74

Fig. 17. View of the Fortress of Scutari by Edward Lear. From *Journal of Travels through Roumeli during an Eventful Period*. London: Henry Colbourn, 1838. 82

Fig. 18. A Venetian Galley of the Fifteenth Century. From Bernhard von Breydenbach, *Peregrinatio in terram sanctam*. Mainz: Erhard Reuwich, 1486. 92

Fig. 19. Venetian Galley under Sail. Drawing by Raphael. Venice: Accademia. 100

MAPS: Toponymy in Cippico

Map. 1. The Lower Adriatic Sea with the Albanian Coast and Scutari. Map © David Bergs, 2014. IX

Map. 2. The Aegean Sea. Map © David Bergs, 2014. X

Map. 3. The Northeastern Mediterranean Sea with Cyprus. Map © David Bergs, 2014. XI

✳

ACKNOWLEDGEMENTS

The work on this volume was supported by a Franklin Research Grant of the American Philosophical Society, a short-term grant of the Gladys Krieble Delmas Foundation for research in libraries and archives outside of Venice and a Faculty Research Grant of the University of Wisconsin-River Falls. I would like to express my gratitude to all these institutions for their much needed sponsorship, and to colleagues, archivists and librarians in Croatia and in Venice's Archivio di Stato and Biblioteca Marciana for their kind assistance. Renate Blumenfeld-Kosinski, Richard Newhauser and Florin Curta supported my quest for funding. Marshall Toman helped with proofreading the text and Brad Caskey, UWRF's CAS Dean, secured the means for that effort, which saved me from many a grammar blunder and unfortunate turn of phrase. Matt Millett assisted with the map work and David Bergs produced the maps. Special thanks are due to the publishers, Eileen Gardiner and Ronald G. Musto, who undertook the painstaking editorial work necessary to bring the manuscript into condition fit to publish.

Some of the issues broached in the introduction were discussed at a seminar on late crusading organized by Renate Blumenfeld-Kosinski at the University of Pittsburgh in November 2012. I would like to thank Renate for the kind invitation to attend and for her hospitality and friendship.

Kiril Petkov
River Falls, WI, September 2014

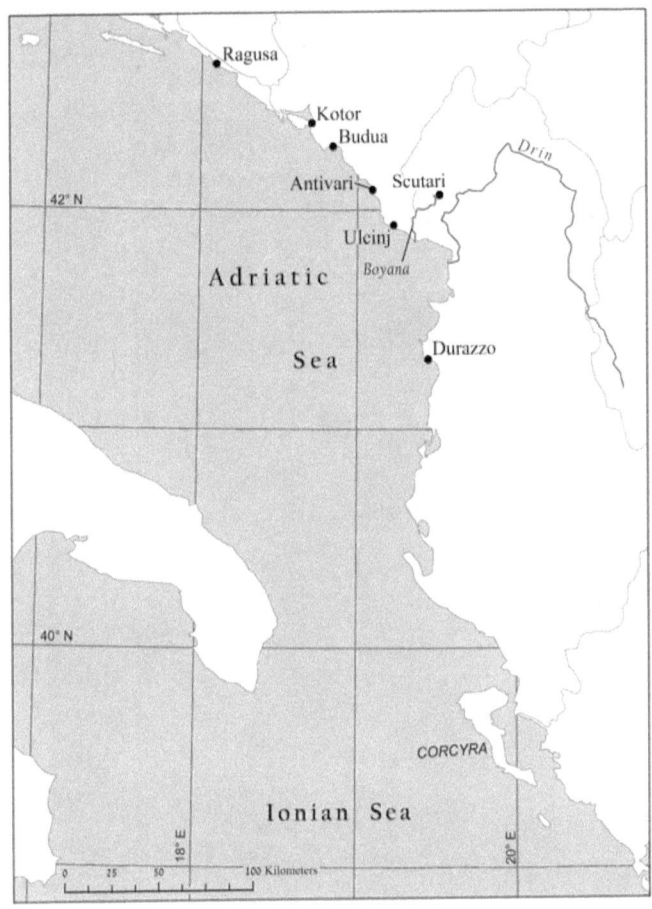

Map. 1. *The Lower Adriatic Sea with the Albanian Coast and Scutari.* Map © David Bergs, 2014.

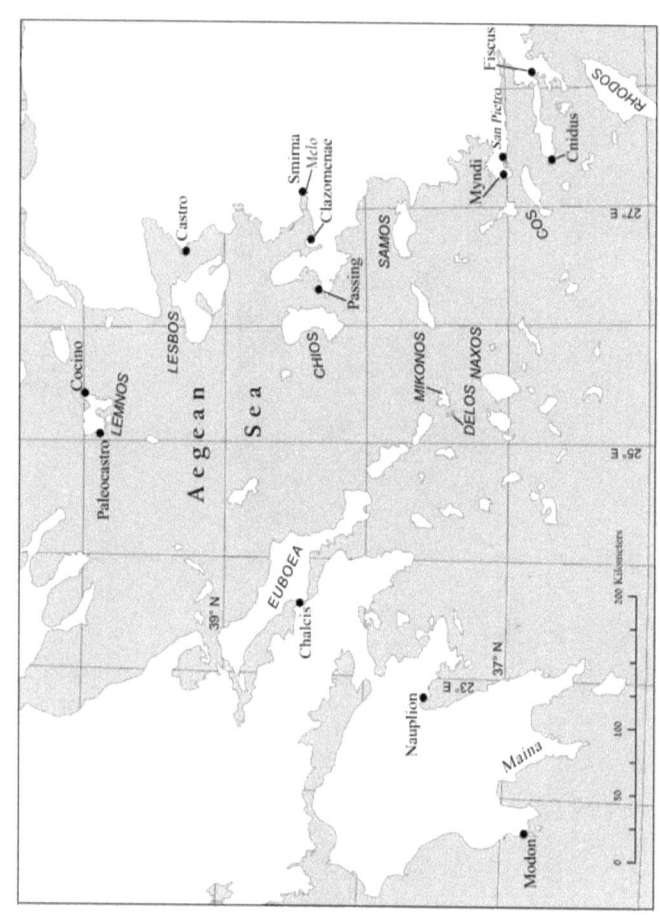

Map. 2. The Aegean Sea. Map © David Bergs, 2014.

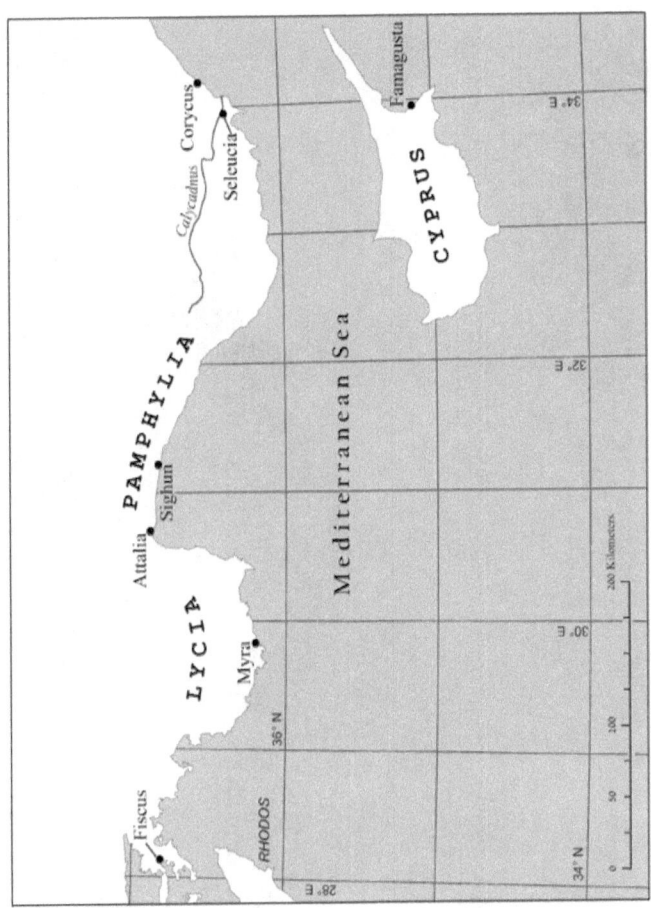

Map 3. The Northeastern Mediterranean Sea with Cyprus. Map © David Bergs, 2014.

Fig. 1. Pietro Lombardo, Portrait statue of Pietro Mocenigo. Funerary Monument of Doge Pietro Mocenigo. SS. Giovanni e Paolo, Venice.

INTRODUCTION: CORIOLANO CIPPICO, HIS WORK AND HIS TIMES

THE AUTHOR

Coriolano Cippico (1425–93), the author of *The Deeds of Commander Pietro Mocenigo*, was a Dalmatian noble of Trogir (Trau), a middling sized town on the eastern coast of the Adriatic Sea.[1] Scion of a patrician household with a long pedigree and possibly Italian origins, Coriolano was raised and educated in the humanist culture of the time. His father, Pietro, was a learned man with antiquarian tastes who associated with Italian and local humanists of note, knew personally the avid antiquarian Ciriaco d'Ancona, collected and copied Latin works and put together a compendium of Roman epitaphs.[2] He was also an active servant of his community and its overlord Venice and a man of action who served as galley captain under Pietro Loredan, the Venetian captain of the sea, in 1431. Coriolano's mother, Peregrina Cega, belonged to an urbanized landholding family and held a village as a fief from Emperor Sigismund in her own right.[3] Shaped in such a family, Coriolano grew

1. This short summary of Cippico's *curriculum vitae* and *cursus honorum* is indebted to D.F. Karaman, "Coriolano Cippico di Traù," *Annuario Dalmatico* 1 (Zadar: Ferrari-Cupilli, 1884), 171–82; Giuseppe Ferrari-Cupilli, *Cenni biografici di alcuni uomini illustri della Dalmazia* (Zadar: S. Artale, 1887), 40–47; Vedran Glico, trans., *Koriolan Cipiko, O Azijskom ratu* (Split: Čakavski Sabor, 1977), introduction, 7-47; Renata Fabri, ed., *Per la memorialistica Veneziana in latino del quattrocento: Filippo da Rimini, Francesco Contarini, Coriolano Cippico* (Padua: Antenore, 1988), introduction, 139–50; and archival material in the historical archives in Zadar and Split as cited in notes below.

2. On Pietro's humanist pursuits, see Giuseppe Praga, "Il codice marciano di Giorgio Begna e Pietro Cippico," *Archivio Storico per la Dalmazia* 13.77 (1932): 210–18; and Bratislav Lučin, "Kodeks Petra Cipika iz 1436," *Živa antika / Antiquité vivante* 57.1-2 (2007): 65–85.

3. Giovanni Lucio, *Delle memorie di Tragurio hora detto Trau* (Venice: Stefano Curti, 1674), 389–90.

to become the perfect embodiment of the Renaissance urban aristocrat and early modern male: no longer a medieval warrior on horseback and a rough castle-dweller but a well-read humanist in command of elegant neoclassical Latin with a keen eye for vestiges of classical antiquity and a local patriot conscious and proud of his cultural background. He was also a town dweller and an absentee landlord with an interest in good husbandry, a trustee of the local cathedral, a diplomat and, just like his father, a leader of men and galley captain serving under Venetian command on behalf of his community.

Although small by the standards of many of the Italian communities across the Adriatic, fifteenth-century Trogir numbered about five thousand souls and boasted well-funded public schools where not just the basic skills of reading and arithmetic required for business ("the abacus") were taught.[4] Coriolano learned his Latin there and possibly some rudimentary Greek as well. At fifteen he went to Padua, whose university was the primary educational establishment in the territorial domain of Venice, Trogir's sovereign. There he polished his classical languages, deepened his knowledge of Roman literature, and developed his rhetorical skill. Padua was the place where several of the prominent humanists of the time had been educated, including Coriolano's illustrious contemporaries Niccolò Perotti (1429-80) and Giovanni Pontano (1426-1503), and later worthies like Giovanni Pico della Mirandola (1463-94), Aldo Manutio the Younger (1547-97), and others.[5] In Padua he also studied nautical matters and military strategy. Back in Trogir after completing his studies, he married

---

4. Lucio, *Delle memorie di Tragurio*, passim, is still the most detailed work on Trogir; see also Paolo Andreis, *Storia della città di Traù* (Split: Hrvatska Stamparija Trumbic, 1908), esp. 170–298. On humanist education in the period see Paul F. Grendler, *Schooling in Renaissance Italy: Literacy and Learning, 1300–1600* (Baltimore: Johns Hopkins University Press, 1989).

5. See Grendler, *Universities*, 225–28.

Fig. 2. Palazzo Cippico, Trogir. Birthplace of Coriolano Cippico. Author

the Venetian noblewoman Giacobina Lodi, who died young, and then married Nicoletta de Andreis. Ten children were born of these marriages, six sons and four daughters. In 1456, aged thirty-one, Coriolano was already a trustee of Trogir's cathedral endowment. He is recorded in the office in 1460, 1477 and 1488 and may have held the position throughout. In the 1450s and 1460s, as an already established local magnate, Coriolano acted as a representative of Trogir to the Venetian Senate. He also served as Trogir's envoy to the Hungarian king, Matthias Corvinus, and the king granted him the privilege of immunity from baronial jurisdiction.[6] Throughout these decades, he found time to refine his credentials as a man of letters among the Venetian nobles with Renaissance tastes, and he associated with leading Italian humanists of the time, including Marcantonio Sabellico and Palladio Fosco.[7] Civic service and literary pursuits were not his only engagement. By 1468 Coriolano was a substantial landlord as well, for his mother had died, and after a suit against his nephew George Ivanishevich in 1472, he inherited her fief of Radosich.

In 1470 the chance came to prove that Cippico was also a man of action in the fashion of his father. Spurred by the debacle of the fall of Negroponte to the Ottoman Turks, the Venetian Senate ordered a naval force led by Pietro Mocenigo to conduct a campaign of retribution. Trogir was asked to contribute a war galley to the Venetian armada, and Cippico was appointed its captain. For the next four years, Coriolano sailed the Aegean and Ionian Seas with Mocenigo in a series of depredations on Ottoman coastal settlements, strengthening the resolve of the Christian Orthodox population on the

6. Andreis, *Storia di Trau*, 287 and n. 2.

7. Cippico's humanist credentials have been discussed by several authors, see for example Marko Špikić, "Razmjene spoznaja o antici u poslanicama hrvatskog humanizma 15. Stoljeća," *Colloquia Maruliana* 18 (April 2009): 63–79.

islands and defending Venetian interests in Cyprus and on the Albanian coasts.[8] Mocenigo valued him highly and entrusted him with several sensitive missions.

True to his literary vocation, Cippico must have kept notes of the campaign's course until its end in 1474. Immediately upon his return, sometime between late 1474 and July 1475, he composed *The Deeds* and dedicated them to Marcantonio Morosini, then Venetian ambassador to the duke of Burgundy.[9] While the treatise added to his humanist standing, the material spoils obtained on the campaign allowed him to demonstrate his civic commitment. With funds from the booty in 1476, Cippico began the construction of a family stronghold on the coast of Trogir, designed to contribute to his commune's commitment to guard against the increasing Ottoman menace in the Adriatic and the Dalmatian hinterland. He funded the construction largely by himself, since the request for support to Trogir's Venetian governor, Troilo Malipiero, which the latter duly relayed to the Senate, was not honored.[10] By late 1481 the family had left their old palazzo in Trogir, still standing today, and moved to the new residence. Besides providing for the family headquarters, spoils from the campaign allowed for the extension of Coriolano's landed estates. In the early 1480s he bought, exchanged and leased out parcels of land, often selling on the condition that cash crops such as wines, grain and fruit-bearing trees would be cultivated on the plots. Apart from revenues from land exploitation and from the liquidation of

8. Cesare Manfroni, "La campagna navale di Pietro Mocenigo," *Rivista marittima* 11.6 (1912): 70–77.

9. As a letter of the humanist Battista Guarini testifies, Cippico was well acquainted with Morosini, see Fabri, *Memorialistica veneziana*, 140–41.

10. Marko Perojević, *Postanak Kaštela* (Sarajevo: Hrvatsko Drustvo Napredak, 1934), 22–65 and especially Giuseppe Praga, "Organizzazione militare in Dalmazia nel quattrocento e la costruzione di Castel Cippico Vecchio di Traù," *Archivio storico per la Dalmazia* 20.119 (1936): 436–72.

the spoils from Mocenigo's campaign, Coriolano drew interest from loans (some of which he extended with money from his wife's dowry) masked as *usufructum*[11] on the land that was used to guarantee the advances. In sum, by the early 1490s Coriolano emerged as a wealthy urban patrician with substantial interests in landed property.[12]

Then a major disaster struck. In 1492, the residence stronghold on the coast caught fire and burned down. Coriolano's spouse Nicoletta lost her life in the blaze. This time around the Venetian Senate promptly extended support, and the castle was restored later that year, but the aged Coriolano's spirits were crushed by the accident. A consolatory letter by Marco Antonio Sabellico testifies to his condition (and informs us that among other things he also wrote poetry).[13] After spending a few more months in the residence, coping with grief, caring for his younger sons and dealing with his landed estate, Coriolano died in 1493. He was buried in Trogir's cathedral, to the right of the main altar. His

11. *Usufructum* is "the right to use and enjoy the property of others without injuring its substance," as defined in Roman law at its early codification and practiced ever since. Its definition and dimensions of application were most extensively discussed in Justinian's Codex, see S. P. Scott, ed. and trans., *The Civil Law including The Twelve Tables, The Institutes of Gaius, The Rules of Ulpian, The Opinions of Paulus, The Enactments of Justinian, and the Constitution of Leo*, 1-2 (Union, NJ: The Lawbook Exchange, 2001), "Title IV: Usufruct," 45 sq.

12. On Cippico's career between 1468 and 1474, see Ivan Pederin, "Koriolan Cippico, njegov odnos sprema Mletaćkoj vlasti i njegove veze s Ugarskom dvorom," *Zbornik Zavoda za povijesne znanosti Istraživačkog centra Jugoslavenske akademije znanosti i umjetnosti* 13 (1983): 191–96. The archival material discussed by Pederin is in the municipal archive of Trogir, currently in the Historical Archive in Zadar, box 68, fasc. 8, where there are 17 documents illustrating Cippico's activities. The documents deserve a more thorough scrutiny, which will be done elsewhere.

13. Andrea Bakotich, "Un carme consolatorio di Marcantonio Sabellico a Coriolano da Traù, (1492)," *Archivio storico per la Dalmazia* 12.69 (1931): 419–49.

INTRODUCTION *

Fig. 3. The Quai of Cippico's Castel Vecchio. From F. Hamilton Jackson, The Shores of the Adriatic: The Austrian Side. *London: John Murray, 1908.*

sons and grandsons continued in the family tradition as town notables, church leaders, Renaissance worthies and fighters against the Ottomans. Fully in the tradition of the house, Coriolano's grandson Alvise commanded a galley in the battle of Lepanto in 1571 and came back with glory and trophies.[14]

*

SUBJECT MATTER

Coriolano's subject matter in *The Deeds* is a Venetian official's war pursuits. But in spite of his extensive ties to Venice and the thrust of his major (or only) literary work, he seems to have been moved more by local civic patriotism, traces of which are clearly visible in *The Deeds*, than by a desire to eulogize the interests of the Republic of Venice, also known as *La Serenissima*. Anecdotal evidence suggests that as a member of Trogir's urban nobility Coriolano staunchly defended his city's autonomy

14. On Cippico's family, see Pietro Cippico's genealogical tree, composed in 1708, *Cronologia dell' Illustrissima casa Cippico dall' Anno 1171*, Trau, ff. 59–66 in the State Archive of Split, Arhiv obitelji Ivčević 11, *Miscellanea, libro X*.

vis-à-vis its Venetian overlords. To him, the alignment with Venice was predicated on fighting the Ottomans rather than on the supposed benefits of Trogir's incorporation into the Venetian imperial domain. It is highly indicative that during the property contest with Ivanishevich, both sides sought the mediation of a local figure, Trogir's vicar Lovrinac, rather than submitting to the jurisdiction of the Venetian governor, Carlo Capello.[15] The local and Venice-based relations of his second wife Nicoletta may have contributed to Coriolano's attitude, as they were not really forthcoming first with her dowry and then with her inheritance. Although focused on extolling the virtues of his hero, the Venetian nobleman and later Doge Pietro Mocenigo, there are indications in *The Deeds* that the treatise was not meant for purely Venetian consumption as were the traditional late medieval and Renaissance chronicles composed by contemporary Venetians. Cippico spent time explaining more than once, for example, typical Venetian practices, such as the auctions of booty assembled during the expedition, that Venetians would have known. He did not spare implicit rebukes of Venetian actions that put the soldiers and commanders of the campaign on the same level as the "barbarian" Ottomans and other Anatolian Muslim population. With the exception of Mocenigo, the bravest, strongest, most dedicated figures in the account are by default non-Venetians, most commonly Dalmatian Slavs. Coriolano also heaps praise on well-arranged political regimes, such as Dubrovnik, to emphasize the advantage of self-governance versus the supposed benefits of Venetian overlordship. In short, Coriolano's work is the encomium of an exemplary Venetian noble but not of Venice the overlord.

  Nonetheless, Cippico's local patriotism was not at the expense of Venice, and the dedication to Morosini explains the author's complex motivation as much as the treatise's contents.

15. Pederin, "Koriolan Cippico," 195.

Marcantonio Morosini (1417–post 1501),[16] was a Venetian noble from the most exclusive circle of the ruling oligarchy, a senator, statesman, magistrate and diplomat, who had an illustrious career that included stints as *podestà* of Brescia, *provveditore* of Cremona and other appointments. He was also a humanist, a marked bibliophile and an art patron. His mission at the Burgundian court, where he resided between May 1474 and November 1475, was in the broad context of negotiating a political treaty between Charles the Bold and Venice, but his objective was quite specific. He was to justify to the duke the Venetian involvement in Cyprus at the expense of the house of Savoy, a loyal ally of the Burgundians. Cippico's ample treatment of the Cypriot affairs in *The Deeds* was right on task, while the remainder of the treatise was in concert with the traditional crusading bent of the Burgundian court. Thus, while the humanist trend of *The Deeds* would have appealed to Morosini's cultured taste, the contents betrayed Cippico's civic preoccupations on the one hand, and aligned well with the two central tasks of Venetian diplomacy, the build-up of the maritime empire and the continuous struggle with the Ottomans, on the other. It was a fine blend indeed.

These narrative preoccupations, perhaps, explain the gist of *The Deeds* in terms of discursive logic. As a humanist, Cippico wrote with a clear set of priorities. Civic duty, loyalty and self-sacrificing service to one's *patria* top the list. These principal — and also transferable — values had not waned with the fall of the ancients. To the contrary, moderns were driven by them even

16. On Morosini, see most recently the extensive article of Giuseppe Gullino, "Morosini, Marcantonio," in *Dizionario Biografico degli Italiani* 77 (Rome: Istituto della Enciclopedia Italiana, 2012), entry accessed online at http://www.treccani.it/enciclopedia/marcantonio-morosini_(Dizionario-Biografico). For Morosini's appointment, see Richard J. Walsh, *Charles the Bold and Italy (1467–1477): Politics and Personnel* (Liverpool: University of Liverpool Press, 2005), 202–4.

more than the Roman and Greek worthies. The four cardinal virtues of the classical citizen —courage, prudence, justice and moderation — follow closely behind the first set of values. The guidance of the one true faith, Christianity, comes third. Last but not least, there is the sense of advancement, refinement and sophistication, the appreciation of a cultured, well-appointed and civilized mode of existence, displayed as much in engineering and artistic capacity as in the more mundane skill of structuring one's everyday cultural and economic circumstances of being in the world. For Cippico narrating Mocenigo's exploits was a vehicle for actualizing the need for expression in the humanist vein, for positioning his historical reality in the flow of a positively unfolding time and for providing a tangible embodiment of the meaning of that reality for him as a Dalmatian Christian nobleman with a specific identity and role in history. The values Coriolano praises in the figure of his paragon Mocenigo are not specifically Venetian; they are universal, applicable to any dedicated servant of a true civic community. In the narrative logic of *The Deeds*, Coriolano's principal hero could have been just as well a member of Trogir's urban elite, a man in the mold of Coriolano's father Pietro, or the author himself.

At first glance, the circumstances that had brought about Mocenigo's expedition were quite clear-cut. The Ottoman territorial advances in the Eastern Mediterranean had dangerously upended the unstable post-Crusade Christian–Muslim balance in the region, in the process affecting the economic and imperial designs of the most active Christian agent in the area, Venice. Acutely conscious of the economic stakes they had in the confrontation the Venetians pursued a policy of accommodation, periodically interrupted by shorter or longer periods of open confrontation with the relentlessly pressing Ottomans. In 1463, a period of hostility opened, marked by a long and exhausting war that lasted until 1479.[17] Despite temporary

17. For the general background, see the rich collection of documents about the relations between Venice, the Ottomans, and Uzun Hasan in

INTRODUCTION ✳

gains, the Christian league orchestrated by Venice and including the papacy, Duke Philip of Burgundy, Hungary and the Albanian lords, was mostly on the defensive and suffered major setbacks in the Balkans and the islands of the Aegean Sea. Worst of all was the loss of Negroponte, the major Venetian possession on Euboea and the fundamental Venetian naval base in the Aegean, in July 1470, a loss that was largely due to the incompetence of the acting Venetian naval commander, Niccolo Canal.[18] Consequently, the leaders of the Serenissima decided to refocus their war effort. Continuing the struggle to counter the Ottomans in the Balkans, where their enemy commanded vastly superior land troops, they deployed their strongest weapon, the navy, and launched an offensive, punitive maritime campaign on the Ottoman coasts. Central and western Mediterranean powers, each with their own agenda, joined the campaign. On August 19, 1470, Pietro Mocenigo (1406–76, doge 1474–76) was appointed supreme naval commander, or captain general of the sea.[19] In late August, he sailed to Euboea with the charge to recover the lost fortress and then to proceed to inflict as much damage on the Ottoman-controlled Levantine coasts as possible. The Serenissima put together a

---

Enrico Cornet, ed., *Le guerre dei Veneti nell'Asia 1470–1474: Documenti cavati dall'archivio ai Frari in Venezia* (Vienna: Tendler, 1856); and Franz Babinger, *Mehmed the Conqueror and His Time*, ed. William C. Hickman, trans. Ralph Mannheim (Princeton, NJ: Princeton University Press, 1978); as well as Halil Inalcik, "The Ottoman Turks and the Crusades, 1451–1522," in Kenneth M. Setton, gen. ed., Harry W. Hazard and Norman P. Zacour, eds., *A History of the Crusades 6. The Impact of the Crusades on Europe* (Madison, WI: University of Wisconsin Press, 1989), 311–53, esp. 325–31; and the thorough discussion and source references of Kenneth M. Setton, *The Papacy and the Levant (1204–1571) 2. The Fifteenth Century* (Philadelphia: American Philosophical Society, 1978, reprint 1997), 298–320.

18. Luigi Fincati, "La perdita di Negroponte (luglio 1470)," *Archivio Veneto* 32.2 (1886): 267–307.

19. Archivio di Stato di Venezia (ASV), Segretario alle voci, Reg. 6, c. 86r.

rather impressive naval force for him, reinforced with aid from its subjects and allies.[20] Trogir, a Venetian possession since 1420 and located within the logistic range of Ottoman naval and ground incursions, supplied a galley, and Coriolano Cippico was appointed its captain. Given his political philosophy, for Coriolano sailing under Mocenigo was not merely executing his city's duty, but an act of active service to his own community and people. The assignment gave him an opportunity to present the confrontation between the aggressive Ottomans, already encroaching on Dalmatia, on the one hand, and the Mediterranean Christians opposing them under the leadership of Venice and her exemplary leader, on the other, as an exercise in civic virtue in the humanist vein.

*

FORM AND THEMES

Writing about the four-year long campaign in which he participated, Cippico likely thought of the form of his work as a *memoria,* or short history of contemporary events, narrated in a straightforward manner, "truer than a prophesy of Apollo," as he put it. Most of the time the narrative follows precisely this contemporary history. But *The Deeds* also offer a strong component of traditional history in the Venetian manner, a mixture of chronicle and *viaggio* accounts, which unfolds geographically and chronologically in space and time. If the frame is traditional, however, the organizing principles are clearly humanist. The work is an encomium directly in the manner of Plutarch's *Lives* of the ancient worthies mixed in with some delicate overtones of an exemplary Christian saint. Cippico's overall frame of reference is progress in the flow of time and the conviction that the "moderns" are no less worthy of admiration than their ancient counterparts. His engine of action, the gallant Commander Pietro Mocenigo, captain of the Gulf, doge of Venice 1474–76,

20. Luigi Fincati, "L'armata di Venezia dal 1470 al 1474," *Rivista marittima* 19 (1886): 384–96 and 20 (1887): 5–183.

is a magistrate, a diplomat, a naval commander and a Homeric speaker of words and doer of deeds. Cippico's professed goal is to highlight Mocenigo's virtues: the qualities of a hero possessing all the positive features of a man exerting himself on behalf of the public good. Combining the gifts of nature with human achievement, Mocenigo led the campaign in the Aegean Sea in the service of the Serenissima in a manner that fused smoothly the cardinal virtues of the archaic hero, the ancient citizen and the true Christian.

The treatise is divided into three books, each covering a stage of the expedition's operations. Mocenigo used the few months remaining in the navigation season of 1470 to move his squadron to Negroponte and assess the chances of recovering the island. He then quartered his ships for winter in several ports of the Venetian Morea. The spring of 1471 was an idle season as well since he awaited the results of the negotiations that the Senate was conducting with Mehmet II (1451–81). In midsummer the talks fell through, and Mocenigo ordered his fleet to the Anatolian shores of the Aegean, where they began depredations on the coastal settlements. By late autumn the galleys returned to Morea and other Venetian-friendly ports in the Archipelago. The attack on the Anatolian coast was renewed early next spring. The years 1472/73 were the peak of the campaign. The fleet went up the coast systematically, attacking and taking Pergamum, several Cilician strongholds, Halicarnassus, Satalia, Clazomenae and Smyrna. With the help of a certain Antonio, a Sicilian and a former Ottoman captive, Mocenigo attempted to sabotage the Ottoman arsenal at Gallipoli. He also served as a relay authority for the Venetian envoys who worked to draw the Karamanian lords and Uzun Hasan (1423–78), the sultan of the Aq Qoyunlu emirate in southern Anatolia, into the struggle against the Ottomans.[21]

21. On Uzun Hasan and his confrontation with the Ottomans, see John E. Woods, The *Aqqunyunlu: Clan, Confederation, Empire* (Salt Lake City: University of Utah Press, 1999), 87–137.

✳ THE DEEDS OF COMMANDER PIETRO MOCENIGO

By late 1473 a new development called off the Anatolian campaign and forced Mocenigo to turn to Cyprus, where a conspiracy struck after the death of King James II (1440–73) on July 10, 1473 and threatened the Venetian hold on the island. With a swift and decisive action and Coriolano Cippico's diplomatic skill, Mocenigo suppressed the revolt and sealed the status of Cyprus as a Venetian colony. The affairs of Cyprus arranged, the remainder of book three contains Mocenigo's involvement, along with the new naval commander, Triadano Gritti, in the repulsion of an Ottoman attempt to seize Scutari, the Albanian stronghold and major Venetian outpost in the western Balkans. In the late summer of 1474, sick with malaria, Mocenigo returned to Venice. The squadron was disbanded, and Coriolano Cippico went home to compose his treatise.

✳

Had his hero lived a century earlier and Cippico had been writing at that time, the account of the expedition would have been a clear-cut crusading narrative. The closest parallel to Mocenigo's actions is the endeavor of Amadeus VI, the "Green Count" of Savoy (1334–83) during his crusading foray of 1366/67.[22] As it was, however, Cippico forsook definitions and catchphrases in his straightforward Latin prose and wove the account from three skeins: classical material for the narrative frame, a throwback to the Venetian tradition of maritime warfare and a scattered but visible theological thread. Each portion merits a brief discussion; against such a backdrop, Cippico's thinking about the historical reality he was enmeshed in will acquire a clearer outline.

The function of the classicist dimension of Cippico's thinking is somewhat puzzling. It is very strong on a narrative level: as an organizing logic, a reference frame, a nomenclature, a system of narrative devices and a comparison benchmark. A few references

22. On Amadeus VI, see Eugene L. Cox, *The Green Count of Savoy: Amadeus VI and Transalpine Savoy in the Fourteenth Century* (Princeton, NJ: Princeton University Press 1967).

suffice to make the point. Cippico's classicism is strongly focused on his agent and main character, the towering figure of Mocenigo, whom he casts in the mold of Plutarch's Julius Caesar. In the preface Cippico expresses his wish that his work would serve as a guide in the genre of the "mirror of princes" to inspire its recipient, nobleman Marcantonio Morosini, to pursue a similarly virtuous life. Cippico's toponymy and ethnonymy are thoroughly ancient, with Plutarch, Pliny the Elder's *Natural History* and Strabo's *Cultural Geography* among his main sources. His ethnographic excurses are very Caesarean. He frequently reflects on vestiges of antiquity found at the areas he discusses.

Conceptually, however, Cippico's classicism is slim where it addresses the gist of the treatise, the juxtaposed, inimical typological opposites: the Venetians with their allies and the Ottomans. The classical "frame" falls short in functioning as a heuristic device. Cippico does apply the generic classical reference of "barbarian" to the Ottoman military and population, but even there he is very restrained. His opposition of "our men" versus the "enemy" leaves a good deal unclear as to the identity of the opponent. Furthermore, his narrative snippets — cameos of references to antiquity or ancient monuments he came to observe in the Anatolian cities seized and ravaged by the Venetian troops — are not causally integrated in his narrative logic. Cippico does not derive any meaning from them. He just drops ethnographic and antiquarian lore for the sake, it seems, of his learned reputation. On only one occasion of scores of such references does he connect a classicizing definition of a people to features of their alleged modern character as a group (in the discussion of Ulcinj, supposedly a foundation of the ancient Colchis) — and even then he does not draw any connection to the narrative logic of his theme for the moment. Nowhere else does he use such inferences to shore up any claim relevant to the characterization or actions of his hero and his troops. Cippico's muted dissatisfaction with the wholesale destruction of vibrant urban quarters still bearing the outlines of their ancient layout, as well as well-tended fields, gardens and orchards, is one other minor element of his classicizing. However, the alleged function of classicism in Renaissance political and military encounters between West and East in the Mediterranean — to make sense of a changed present with the means of ancient thought-models — is underdeveloped, to say the least.[23]

It is difficult to determine to what extent that attitude depends on the second main line of Cippico's representation and perception of the expedition: the material side of the Venetian reprisals. Despite its coastal bases, subject towns and island possessions, the Venetian maritime empire in the eastern Mediterranean was primarily a commercial entity, while its principal opponent, the Ottoman empire, was overwhelmingly a territorial polity. Since the Venetian empire's inception, raiding enemy coastal settlements or those of people of neutral affiliation, looting, sacking and pillaging, had been the traditional Venetian mode of warfare. For the most part, capturing and holding strongholds as a matter of state policy was considered when such strongholds supported Venetian trade lines and could serve as strategic entrepôts and naval bases. The acquisition of the *terraferma* and large islands in the Mediterranean, such as Cyprus, began to change that strategy after the beginning of the 1400s, but the general premise applied. Mocenigo's expedition was no exception from that rule. Cippico makes it clear that his hero's commission was to distract Mehmet II from carrying on the momentum of Negroponte across the Adriatic, a fear that proved justified by the end of the decade with the Ottoman assault on Otranto.[24]

23. As argued by Margaret Meserve, *Empires of Islam in Renaissance Historical Thought* (Cambridge, MA: Harvard University Press, 2008). Meserve does not discuss Cippico's work. See also James Hankins, "Renaissance Crusaders: Humanist Crusade Literature in the Age of Mehmed II," *Dumbarton Oaks Papers* 49 (1995): 111–207.

24. Alessio Bombacci, "Venezia e la impresa Turca di Otranto," *Rivista Storica Italiana* 66 (1954): 159–203.

Whether that could be done in the manner the Venetians envisaged it is questionable, but Mocenigo did what it took to prove that Venice still ruled the high seas and could turn that advantage to good profit. City after city on the Anatolian coast, defended by a token Janissary garrison, was attacked by surprise and taken over, often after a bloody struggle with the defenders. The Venetian troops then sacked and burned the settlements, in the process destroying several of the ancient remains so dear to Cippico. They killed those who resisted, enslaved whoever fell into their hands and took the loot to the galleys. Particularly brutal was the seizure and looting of Smyrna: the ancient, prosperous city was thoroughly ravaged, sacked, and burned to the ground, reduced to ashes in a few hours, as the author reports with unmitigated regret. Afterwards, Cippico is careful to explain in detail, the spoils were properly apportioned, officials elected and auctions took place where captives, carpets, cloth, spice and other precious goods were sold and carried off for further distribution in the capital or in other markets. The technical details of the loot and the auctions were hardly of importance for the success of Mocenigo's mission and would have been quite familiar to the contemporary Venetian public. Yet Cippico felt compelled to allot them ample space in the account, which again suggests that he was writing with wider audience in mind. In addition, that part may have been as high on the mind of the troops as it was prominent in the account, with the added emphasis of a culture fascinated with the technical dimensions of legalizing property.

Religion threads throughout the narrative, though Cippico clearly does not conceive of the expedition in purely religious terms. Several moments in the text do recall some of the traditional features of crusade narratives. It is intriguing, moreover, that he left out the fact that the expedition was part of the protracted, sixteen-year struggle with the Ottomans (1463–79) in the course of which Venice had entered a holy league with other Mediterranean powers, an uneasy alliance blessed by the pope and strengthened by the participation of a naval squadron outfitted and maintained by the papacy. Given Cippico's stress on the "eyewitness account" mode of writing — a feature that seems to have permeated Venetian mentality of the time and stretched to all modes of discourse, narrative, art and architecture[25] — the omission is not decisive. The account abounds in religious references packaging the narrative in an age-old fashion. For Cippico, for example, the Ottomans are "the common enemy of the Christian religion." Their religious affiliation is crystal clear. The province of Asia (Asia Minor or Anatolia) is inhabited by the "barbarian infidel people of Muhammad's sect." The Muslim–Christian distinction runs deep. It was an ontological reality, which even the dogs in an Anatolian town acknowledged, according to Cippico, by distinguishing between Christian and Muslim, and favoring the Christians. On a formal level, although the Christian league that would qualify the expedition as a crusade is not mentioned, the implicit acknowledgement is there. In a meeting with the papal legate and naval commander Cardinal Oliviero Carafa in 1472, Mocenigo stated that the Venetian Senate had done much for the Christian faith and for liberty of the Church. The legate acknowledged the effort on account of the Christian religion and in defense of the Christian people from the madness of the barbarians and offered his prayers for Mocenigo's success.

When it came to firing up the spirit of his fighters during the siege of Satalia, Mocenigo extolled the troops to fight for the Christian faith, the glory of Venice and the rich spoils awaiting them, in that order. Within a classicist device — the direct speech

---

25. On the "eyewitness" trend in fifteenth-century Venetian culture see, above all, the works of Patricia Fortini Brown, *Venetian Narrative Painting in the Age of Carpaccio* (New Haven: Yale University Press, 1988); *Venice and Antiquity: The Venetian Sense of the Past* (New Haven: Yale University Press, 1996); as well as *Art and Life in Renaissance Venice* (New York: Prentice Hall, 1997).

— Cippico has Antonio, the Sicilian youth who attempted to sabotage the arsenal at Gallipoli, accuse the Ottoman sultan of illegally taking over the states of other lords; he lambasts the sultan's bad faith and his oppression of his subjects, and Antonio condemns his drive to extinguish Christianity, the one and only pure religion. During the siege of Scutari, the Venetian commander Antonio Loredan responded to an offer to surrender by stating that he put his faith and his loyalty to his country above any riches the Ottomans would have heaped upon him. At the same siege, Loredan exhorted the defenders to fight for the one immortal God and out of loyalty to Venice, which was sure to reward them appropriately, and called on them to think about their *virtù* and the Christian religion and to defend their country and children and wives from the cruel barbarian. In another episode, as Mocenigo stopped in Ragusa on his way home to receive medical attention, he was treated by the citizens "almost as a god who had descended from heaven to defend the Christian faith." Despite the anachronistic humanist conflation, the drift is clear. And, as Cippico repeats over and over again, animated by the antique-like spirit of the common good, Mocenigo was not driven by vain ambition as the ancient worthies had been, but by true love for the Christian religion and for his country.

In sum, mixed as the messages are, the presence of the religious motivation is indisputable. Is it, however, an explanatory presence? Even with the strong classical frame organizing the narrative and the quite visible contours of the discourse of the crusade wrapped around it, the faith-inspired moral thread in Cippico's account is very thin. On the face of it, Mocenigo and his troops were more base robbers than spirited defenders of righteous Christendom. The principal reason for that impression is the nature of the military-political thread in the account, a feature that modern scholarship is inclined to see as taking over the place of religious motivation under the pressure of the classical model. As evidenced, so far as Coriolano's narrative is concerned, the claim is somewhat overrated. Nevertheless, the observation does point to the deficiencies of his political discourse. The latter is so loaded as to undermine the very notion of righteous providential politics that lay at the heart of crusade. A pure theological frame would strongly suggest a radical divide between Muslim and Christian. The Ottoman–Venetian encounter here is turned into a case *sui generis* in order to sidestep the rather cozy relations with other Muslim powers entertained by Venice and other Christian states, the papacy included.[26] That typological, conceptual difference is confirmed by the explicit reference of the papal legate to the Venetians' killing, despoiling and destroying of Ottoman subjects as a supreme example of Mocenigo's *virtù*. The supposedly rigid, ontological boundary that Coriolano occasionally draws around the camps of "us" versus "them" in order to create a dichotomy that fits the paradigm of providential politics is fundamentally flawed on several counts.

First, there is the humanist political discourse about the Ottoman advance as an illicit, illegitimate, tyrannical power grab based on sheer military might. Narrative snippets imply just that. Antonio, the former Ottoman captive and would-be saboteur of the arsenal of Gallipoli, states as much in a spirited harangue before the Ottoman sultan. The speech is

26. The Western Mediterranean Christian nations have always maintained good relations with Mamluk Egypt; Venice was foremost among them, but so did the Genoese, the Catalans, the Provençals, the Cypriots, and other trading nations, even the Knights Hospitaller of Rhodes. The disruptive entry of the Ottomans pushed Venice to seek allies, and they found them in another fifteenth-century Anatolian Muslim power, the Karamanids. The popes, for their part, had insisted on a largely futile embargo of Egypt since the early crusading era, but joined the commercial powers in their rapprochement with the Karamanids. See Paolo Preto, *Venezia e i Turchi* (Florence: Sansoni, 1975; 2nd edition, Viella, 2013); Stefano Carboni, *Venice and the Islamic World, 828–1797* (New York: Metropolitan Museum of Art, 2007); and Setton, *The Papacy and the Levant (1204–1571)*, passim.

a direct derivative of Gaius Mucius Scaevola's address of the Clusian king Lars Porsena, but it is detached from its classical milieu as Cippico elaborated on the issue numerous times in the narrative. The point would have been legitimate had not Coriolano himself portrayed the western Christian concepts of political relations in precisely such power terms. In his dealings with the conspirators of Cyprus, for example, Coriolano has Mocenigo respond to their argument for the legitimacy of Charlotte's claim to the kingdom, as opposed to that of his protégée Caterina Cornaro, with a phrase that is an exact parallel to Antonio's accusations against the Ottomans, namely that "kingdoms do not pass under the jurisdiction of princes through legal formularies or contests in court, but through feats of arms and valor" — a perfect example of embracing the principle of "might makes right" that was used to underscore the illegitimacy of Ottoman empire building. The political reality trumps the humanist discourse of motives, and it could hardly have been otherwise, given that Venice had just cobbled together a territorial empire on the *terraferma* herself, for no other reason but because it could.

Second, there is Cippico's explanation of the motivation behind the military confrontation between Christian and Muslim. The allegations that the Ottomans wanted to suppress the Christian faith aside, the structural reason for the clash is that Venice was under attack and had to defend itself and its subject and allies. Antonio Loredan's words to the defenders of Scutari, "fight for your land, wives and children," are exactly to that effect. And yet, at the Venetian siege of Satalia, it was the locals who fought for "country, freedom, wives and children," whereas, according to Cippico, the Venetian troops fought for glory and out of greed. It is quite interesting that a writer as skillful as Cippico could literally use the same phrase, apparently unmindful of the mirror image it creates and the claim it undermines.

The third flaw is the author's analysis of the conduct and behavior of the opposing sides. Cippico certainly scores a point for his party as he narrates how the Ottoman garrisons, after proudly professing their loyalty to their master, quickly gave up their charges in exchange for safe conduct. Such snippets amply support the perception of the Ottoman polity as a tyranny and are a nice counterpoint to the loyalty of steadfast defenders of Christian strongholds who kept the faith to their Venetian overlord. However, according to Cippico's own account, more than once Venetian troops pursued scorched-earth tactics, burning, killing and destroying indiscriminately. They were appropriately defined by a Muslim woman from Smyrna as "barbarian enemies." It is Cippico, of course, who puts the words into the mouth of the woman, but he also leaves them without commentary. He also strengthens the message with an explicit regret that a city so noble, so well-appointed and with such a past was razed to the ground by none other than the Venetian defenders of Christianity.

Fourth — and here the flaw is author-specific — whatever the alleged origins of his family and its contemporary affiliation, Cippico was a Dalmatian Slav and felt like one. His political discourse is destabilized by his nascent nationalism. Cippico was very sensitive to the presence of Slavs — Dalmatians, Slavonians, Bosnians and other Balkan Slavs — in the encounters he describes, and he has a knack for highlighting their origin, their prowess and their skill, no matter to which side they belonged. And the facts on the ground were that men of Slavic extraction served both sides, since the Slavs who affiliated with Venice and western Christendom had an exact counterpart in the Slavs who served the sultan and Islam (as Janissaries indeed, but still clearly identifiable by their origin). On that level, the "enemy" was "us," for to Cippico a Slav was a Slav first and foremost, and only then a Venetian subject and ally or an Ottoman warrior converted to Islam.

Together, these flaws reflect a breakdown of the difference between Christian and Muslim that could sustain the moral high ground on which the political morality of the narrative supposedly rested. Rather than reinforcing the ontology inherent in the religious dichotomy, the narrative suggests an overlapping, hybrid political morality. Cippico's humanist discourse is thus hard put to carry its own ideological message and destabilizes the entire fabric of providential politics that would have justified the thrust of his version of the encounter. His account reflects a period during which the moral certainty of the traditional crusade had given way to a confused double standard through which the paradigm of encountering the "other" was incorporated into Western political practice. The aliens of earlier ages looked all too similar in this fifteenth-century clash in the eastern Mediterranean. Cippico had no doubts and no soft spot for the Ottomans and clearly saw them as a force bent on destroying his world, but he certainly had trouble thinking of the encounters as a clean-cut clash of two alien worlds.

*

THIS EDITION

The editio princeps of the *Deeds* was published by Bernard Pictor, Erhardt Ratdolt, and Peter Löslein under the title *Petri Mocenici imperatoris gesta*.[27] An unidentified *litteratus* at the court of Urbino made a handwritten copy for Duke Federico soon thereafter, committing many scribal errors in the process.[28] An early modern reprint appeared in Basel in a collection printed by Rudolf Wintner and containing Conrad Venger's *De bello inter Sigismundum Archistrategum Austriae et Venetos* and Michele Coccinio's *De bellis italicis* in 1544. Another Basel edition was collated with Laonicus Chalkokondilas' *History of the Turks* in

27. Venice: Bernard Pictor, 1477.
28. Now in the Vatican Library, Cod. Vaticano Urbinate lat. 923, described by Cosimo Stornaiolo, *Codices Urbinate Latini* 2 (Rome: Vatican Press, 1912), cols. 43–108.

1556. The treatise was prepared in Venice by Coriolano's grandson Giovanni Cippico and printed by Antonio Rampazetti in 1594 under the title *De bello asiatico Coriolani Cippici Dalmatae Traguriensis Libri Tres*. The last early modern edition was published in Strasbourg in 1611 in a volume printed by Ludvig Zetzen and containing Pietro Giustiniani's *History of Venice* as well. The only modern edition of the Latin text is by Renata Fabbri, *Per la memorialistica veneziana in latino del Quattrocento. Filippo da Rimini, Francesco Contarini, Coriolano Cippico*.[29]

Coriolano's treatise appeared in Italian in 1570 in a Venetian edition by Domenico and Giovanni Battista Guerra, made by an anonymous translator in a rather free rendition under the title *Delle cose fatte da M. Pietro Mocenico capitano generale di mare della serenissima signoria di Venezia libri tre*. Other translations into Italian were made in 1594 and 1794. Finally, Jacopo Morelli produced a new Italian translation which, although superior and truer to the Latin text than all previous versions, took a few liberties with the text itself (Venice: Carlo Palese, 1796). The only translation into a modern language is the competent rendition in Croatian by Vedran Gligo, ed. and trans., *Koriolan Cippico, O Asijsklom Ratu: Petri Mocenici Imperatoris Gesta (De bello asiatico)* (Split: Čakavski Sabor, 1977), with an introduction about the literary milieu and reception of Coriolano's work.

The history of printings and translations testifies to the popularity of *The Deeds*; no less telling is their reception by leading historians of the period, both in the traditional and in the humanist vein. Cippico's work was the principal source of the chief Venetian authority for the later fifteenth century, the annals of Domenico Malipiero, and for the more conceptual work of the official humanist historian, Marcantonio

---

29. Padua: Antenore, 1988.

Sabellico.[30] Echoes of *The Deeds* reverberate through scores of Venetian amateur histories composed at the turn of the fifteenth century and beyond.

This translation is based on Renata Fabbri's edition, with reference to Bernard Pictor's printing. The translation is as close as possible to Coriolano's elegant, concise Latin. This principle may have led, I am afraid, to not a few rather clumsy turns of phrase. But then, aiming for an English text true to the word and spirit of the original, I could not hope to match the skill of the famed Latinist upon whom contemporary humanists had heaped praise. Scholars with a command of Latin will be able to make their own conclusions about the quality of the translation. For the rest of the modern readership I hope that I have provided a straightforward narration, in a manner that the author himself may have approved.

✻

---

30. Domenico Malipiero, *Annali veneti dall'anno 1457 al 1500*, Francesco Longo and Agostino Sagredo, eds., in *Archivio storico italiano* 7 (1843); Marcantonio Sabellico, *Historiae rerum venetarum ab urbe condita* (Venice: Torresani, 1487).

Fig. 4. Pietro Lombardo. Funerary Monument of Doge Pietro Mocenigo. SS. Giovanni e Paolo, Venice.

THE DEEDS OF COMMANDER PIETRO MOCENIGO IN THREE BOOKS

DEDICATION

To the Most Excellent Messer Marcantonio Morosini, Ambassador of Venice to the Most Illustrious Duke of Burgundy, Greetings from Coriolano Cippico

Ever since I was appointed galley captain in the armada led by His Excellency Lord Pietro Mocenigo, most happy commander of the most serene signoria of Venice, against Mehmet, lord of the Turks, you have asked me insistently to write down with diligence all that occurred during that expedition, enjoining me to account for everything in words truer than the prophecies of Apollo's oracle.

To please you, therefore, I have recorded everything that was accomplished by the said Commander Mocenigo in the period of four years during which he held the admiralty and I served as captain. I am now sending you the booklet in which I have described those events. I am certain that by reading it you will come to admire the excellent virtues of the commander no less than his valorous deeds. Moreover, you will come to hold as hollow the claims of those who assert that these days of ours are sterile and have not produced the kind of valiant men that proliferated in ancient times and that, with the aging of the world, all things tend to degenerate.

That those are false claims is clearly demonstrated by the fact that if among the Greeks and the Romans there were many who were great and illustrious through particular virtues, what are we to say about Commander Mocenigo, on whom kindly nature had imparted all of her blessings? I will leave aside his noble stock, his grave demeanor informed by regal dignity, his eloquence, and all other gifts of nature; but I will not forsake to describe the qualities of the man. For his ways are impeccable and his life that of a saint: magnanimous in war, clement toward the vanquished, severe and harsh to rebels, pleasant with loyal subjects, just with everyone, guarded with the means of others and generous with what belongs to him, a man who makes do easily without the pleasures and comforts of life. Is it not reasonable, therefore, not only to compare but to place him above ancient admirals and commanders and give thanks to our times for producing such a great man?

Artists study closely paintings and sculptures fashioned by those who excel in their craft to become as good as the masters. I would suggest that you endeavor to emulate the ways and the life of that outstanding commander and excellent prince and admiral. Adorned with virtues as rare as his, you would be worthy of pursuing the highest honors and dignities of your homeland and, ultimately, the office of prince itself.

Farewell.

BOOK ONE

[1470]

NEWS CAME TO VENICE that the Ottoman, the prince of the Turks,[1] had moved to attack the island of Euboea and the city of Chalcis with a large force by land and sea and in a few days had seized it.[2] The islands and cities of Greece, frightened by the great multitude of Ottomans (for the Ottoman fleet exceeded three hundred vessels, while their land forces numbered more than hundred and twenty thousand soldiers) placed their hopes in flight rather than valor. Considering the state of affairs, the city filled with fear and began to despair of her own safety. Solemn processions were ordered and speeches were heard, both in public and in private, of how to ensure the salvation of the republic. In the end, it was considered best to elect a seasoned commander who would strengthen with his authority

1. Mehmet the Conqueror (1444–46 and 1451–81), son of Murat II. The most successful and expansionist of the early Ottoman rulers, he took over Constantinople in 1453 and then proceeded to put an end to the remaining Christian principalities in the Balkans (Serbia in 1459, Morea 1458–60, Bosnia in 1463, Albania 1466–78), established a presence in the Crimea in 1475, placed Wallachia under Ottoman suzerainty in 1464 and annexed the domain of the Karamanian lords in Anatolia in 1464–73. The best discussion on him is still Franz Babinger, *Mehmed the Conqueror and His Time*, ed. William C. Hickman, trans. Ralph Mannheim (Princeton, NJ: Princeton University Press, 1978).

2. Euboea is the second-largest Greek island and the largest one in the Aegean Sea. It lies across the Euboean Gulf from Attica and Boetia, and Chalcis is its main settlement. The island was seized and ruled by assorted Frankish barons after the Fourth Crusade in 1204. Since the fourteenth century Venice had expanded its presence and control of the island's economy, and in 1390 it became Venetian possession. Mehmet II's expedition was launched in the summer of 1470; and the city of Chalcis fell on July 12, 1470, largely due to the inept action of the Venetian commander, Niccolo da Canal.

the fallen and weakened spirits of the subjects and allies, and who would oppose the enemy with a virtuous and courageous disposition. The Senate decreed to recall Commander Niccolo Canal.[3] In his stead it unanimously appointed to the task Pietro, scion of the renowned family Mocenigo, whose kindred had been among the patrician families of the city since its inception. Many of them were renowned commanders, men adorned with the glory of naval battles. The most recent among these was Tommaso Mocenigo, illustrious doge

3. Niccolo Canal (1415–83) was a Venetian patrician, man of letters, public servant and diplomat. His service included a term as head of the Council of Ten, captain of Brescia and several diplomatic appointments, among them missions to France, Constantinople and the negotiations of the Peace of Lodi. In spite of his lack of maritime experience and known indecisiveness, he was elected captain general of the sea in January 1469 and placed in charge of the defense of the Venetian possessions in the Aegean, but he fared poorly. His initial success in sacking the city of Aenos in 1469, where the Venetian troops took thousands of captives, including Greek Christian women, and a few Lydian settlements, incited Mehmet II's retaliation campaign against Euboea. Facing a superior Ottoman armada, Canal retired to Candia (Crete). Unopposed, the Ottoman fleet then invested the western shores of Euboea and constructed a pontoon bridge that connected the island to the mainland to allow a large land force led by Mehmet II in person to cross over. On the eve of the crossing, on July 11, 1470, after much tarrying, Canal's sizable squadron suddenly appeared to the north of the bridge. Enjoying a favorable wind and tide and catching the Turks unawares, Canal could have destroyed the pontoon and enemy fleet. Instead, he kept his armada idle against the urging of his galley captains and the desperate signals of the besieged Chalcidians, and the Ottomans continued their assault on Chalcis. On the next day, July 12, before Canal finally decided to move, the exhausted city fell. The island remained in Ottoman hands until 1830. Canal was recalled, tried before the Senate, and despite calls for severe punishment, was only sentenced to perpetual exile in Portogruaro. See di Ventura, "Niccolo Canal," in *Dizionario biografico degli Italiani* (DBI) 17 (1974), entry now available online at http://www.treccani.it/enciclopedia/nicolo-canal_(Dizionario-Biografico) with extensive bibliography.

of Venice, whose great deeds made him worthy of heaven and immortality.[4] Messer Pietro himself was highly esteemed for his godly life and the integrity of his faith as much as he was for his indomitable spirit and experience in warfare. He had always enjoyed the reputation of a valorous commander, a distinguished senator and a great citizen.[5]

After accepting the supreme command, Mocenigo quickly had a galley armed and a few days later left Venice without further delay. Navigating under favorable conditions, in a short time he reached Greece. There, given the great gravity of the matter, he traversed all the cities and islands of that province, lifted the frightened and suffering spirits of subjects and confederates, and comforted the afflicted with his presence and his words. He assured them that the Ottoman had taken Chalcis not through deeds of valor but through a ruse. He had sailed forth like a thief from an ambush and assaulted those who were not prepared; in a brief while, however, the Ottoman would be forced to turn back his thoughts and his troops to preserve what belonged to him rather than subjecting to depredations what belonged to others. After so consoling the spirits of all these peoples, he departed for Euboea. As he entered the straights that separate the island from the mainland, he came to Commander Niccolo Canal. Canal had a multitude of galleys

4. Tommaso Mocenigo, doge 1414–23, was a *provveditore* of the Venetian fleet in 1381, captain general of the sea in 1396, and duke of Candia in 1403. He also served as Venetian envoy on several diplomatic missions.

5. Pietro Mocenigo (1406–76), doge 1474–76, dedicated his early years to commercial activity and held minor offices. His active career began in 1443 as galley captain in the Adriatic fleet, then one of the *savvi* of the *terraferma*, captain of the convoy of Beirut, member of the Council of Ten, ducal counselor, *avogador di Comun*, and diplomatic envoy, before he was elected captain general of the sea on August 19, 1470. See Giuseppe Gullino, "Pietro Mocenigo," *Dizionario Biografico degli Italiani* 75 (Rome: Istituto della Enciclopedia Italiana, 2011), entry online at http://www.treccani.it/enciclopedia/pietro-mocenigo_(Dizionario-Biografico).

under him and had given orders to approach Chalcis. He prepared to attack and capture the city, hoping to try his luck and to find a way to recover what had been lost.

Once he had caught sight of Mocenigo's galley, Canal realized from the standards it was flying that his successor had arrived. He left his own ship, descended into a skiff and joined Mocenigo on board his vessel. The two saluted and embraced. Then Canal said: "You can see, my lord commander, the large fleet that I have assembled from all over and how I have arranged everything necessary to attack the city. I have assigned positions to all captains and commanding officers and put everything in good order. There is every hope that you will be able to recover the city. Therefore, I surrender the high command to you. Continue what I have begun, and without doubt you will succeed in taking back the city."

But Mocenigo, thinking more about the public good than of acquiring accolades for himself, as well as being new to the situation and ignorant of the designs of his predecessor, not wanting to upend things, replied: "Niccolo, better proceed with what you have begun, as it appears to be for the common good. I will be at your disposal, be it as a colleague or as subordinate, and I will do whatever you charge me with, so that you can recover the lost city." To this Niccolo responded that he would not want to do anything since he was no longer in charge and the command was not his. Mocenigo realized, however, that Niccolo spoke for the sake of appearances and was not sincere, and the whole enterprise had no chance of success. For two galley captains who had led the land assault had been killed and their troops turned to flight, while some of the galleys, which had taken artillery hits, had their hulls fractured and barely floated on the water.

Therefore, losing hope for recovering the city, he dismissed the vessels that were inadequately armed. And because summer was already over and winter approached, he took the remaining long galleys to the ports of the Peloponnese. He decided to wait there for the coming of the new year and bide his time until summer, when he would be able to engage in a worthy pursuit that would make up for the damage suffered with the loss of Euboea. With this in mind, he ordered that the galleys that needed repair be attended to and sent the others to the islands of the Archipelago to instill confidence and courage in the souls of the Venetian subjects there.

[1471]

WHILE ALL THIS was taking place in Greece, in Venice two legates of the fleet were elected, Messer Marino Malipiero and Messer Alvise Bembo.[6] Both were mature men, expert in naval affairs. They were charged with advising the commander in conducting the matters of war. As soon as spring was in the offing, the two had their galleys armed and departed without delay to join the commander and discuss together with him what was to be arranged during the summer to harass the enemy and defend the domain of the republic. For his part, King Ferdinand of Naples, according to the alliance concluded with him, sent another ten armed galleys under the command of Rechaiense to assist the commander in the war against the Turks.[7]

---

6. Marino Malipiero (1400/1403–78) began his political career in 1435/36 as member of the Council of Forty and then served in a variety of judicial and administrative magistracies, among which captain and *podestà* of Mestre, Ravenna and Verona, and member of the Council of Ten and the Small Council of the republic. In the early 1440s he took a series of appointments in the naval forces, which made him a suitable figure for the post of *provveditore* with Mocenigo. Not much is known about the career of Alvise Bembo.

7. Ferdinand of Naples (1458–94), natural son of Alfonso V of Aragon, joined the anti-Ottoman league between Venice and the papacy

Meanwhile the Ottoman, the prince of the Turks, was concerned, I suppose, that the conquest of Euboea would provoke the Christian princes to align themselves in war against him. He tried to put things to rest by making peace with Venice — or sought to prolong matters until the atrocities committed at the conquest of Chalcis faded away — through the assistance and services of his Christian stepmother, the daughter of Despot George, the late ruler of the Serbians.[8] At the instigation of her stepson she sent to Venice the most trusted among her servants, intimating that the Venetians should send ambassadors to the Turk and assuring them that if they did, they would have a peace treaty that would suit them. Two envoys were appointed, Niccolo Cocco and Francesco Cappello. They boarded a galley and first sailed to meet with the despot's daughter, who resided in a village in Macedonia, which had been granted to her by her stepson. After talking to the woman, from there they proceeded by land to Constantinople,

---

and sent a squadron under the Catalan noble Requesnes that aided Mocenigo's exploits.

8. Mara Brankovich (1420–76 or 1487) daughter of Despot George Brankovich (1427–56), married Sultan Murat II (1421–44 and 1446–51) in 1435 and was thus Mehmet's stepmother. She was very active as intermediary between her husband and son, on the one hand, and her father and other Christian potentates, on the other. After Mehmet's accession, she retired to her estate of Strumitza but continued her efforts on behalf of Mehmet's Christian subjects and sponsored monastic foundations. According to Donald Nicol, her principal residence was at Jezhevo, near modern Dafni, in Mount Athos. See Donald M. Nicol, *The Byzantine Lady: Ten Portraits 1250–1500* (Cambridge: Cambridge University Press, 1994), 110–19; see also Zara Gavrilović, "Women in Serbian Politics, Diplomacy, and Art at the Beginning of Ottoman Rule," in Elizabeth Jeffreys, ed., *Byzantine Style, Religion, and Civilization: In Honor of Sir Steven Runciman* (Cambridge: Cambridge University Press, 2007), 72–90. For a recent discussion of her life and career, see Mihailo Popović, *Mara Branković: Eine Frau zwischen dem christlichen und dem islamischen Kulturkreis im 15. Jahrh.* (Mainz: Rutzen, 2010).

where they saluted the prince of the Turks according to custom and opened negotiations via interpreters. Unable to agree on the terms of the peace, the envoys sent letters to the Senate, detailing the conditions demanded by the Turk. The Venetians rejected the conditions, and the Senate decreed to recall the ambassadors. In the meantime, Francesco Cappello contracted fever and died. Niccolo, the other envoy, got to the island of Lemnos on a fishing boat, and from there a Venetian galley brought him to Crete.[9]

By the time the envoys had travelled, conducted negotiations, and sent and received letters, summer had passed. And while this was going on, the commander was anxious to undertake some endeavor worthy of his stance and the glory of his ancestors, but dissuaded by the legates, he refrained from action. The fear was that the barbarian enemy, thus offended, would harm the noble and innocent ambassadors. As winter approached, the captain of the royal fleet sailed back to Naples. The legates Marin Malipiero and Alvise Bembo were recalled home as well. Losing hope in settling the matter with the Turk, the Venetians began to prepare for war in the coming year. Envoys were sent out, first to the pope, then to King Ferdinand, exhorting them to mobilize and commit effort and men against the common enemy and pernicious plague of the Christian religion. The pope accepted the envoys sympathetically and committed himself and his men.[10] King Ferdinand was also excited to join with his forces the next year.

9. For these events, see Kenneth M. Setton, *The Papacy and the Levant, 1204–1571*, vol. 2, *The Fifteenth Century* (Philadelphia: Memoirs of the American Philosophical Society, 1978), 307–11. Francesco Cappello died in Constantinople, and Cocco was ordered to remain on Corfu until June 1472 to relay information to Marco Aurelio, another Venetian envoy who left for Constantinople accompanied by Theodore, Mara Brankovich's emissary, but did not proceed farther than Corfu.

10. Pope Sixtus IV (Francesco della Rovere) (1471–84).

The commander, for his part, sent envoys with letters to the grand master of the Order [of Hospitallers[11]] in Rhodes and to the king of Cyprus to prepare for war in the coming spring

Fig. 5. Rhodes. From Hartmann Schedel, Nuremberg Chronicle. *Nuremberg: Anton Koberger, 1493.*

and to send the galleys they owed according to the treaty.[12] Then he sailed with the fleet to the Aegean islands, fearing that the enemy might seize the opportunity and attack allies and subjects there, for many of their fortresses are weak and

11. The best work on the Hospitallers after their establishment on Rhodes remains Anthony Luttrell, *The Hospitaller State on Rhodes and its Western Provinces* (Aldershot: Ashgate, 1999) and his *Studies on the Hospitallers after 1306: Rhodes and the West* (London: Variorum, 2007); more recently, see the concise survey of Jonathan Riley-Smith, *Hospitallers: The History of the Order of St John* (London: Hambledon, 2003).

12. Grand Master Giovanni Battista Orsini (1467–76) and James II of Lusignan (1463–73). Both were allied with Venice against the Ottomans, and James II had married the Venetian noblewoman Caterina Cornaro in 1468.

inadequately armed. Sojourning in the area with the armada, he learned that a wealthy settlement in Ionia had been left defenseless. It is called Passing by the locals and is situated on the mainland opposite the island of Chios.[13] There congregate the wares from almost all Asian provinces, and from there they are shipped over to Chios. That city is now under the Genoese, together with the entire island, and serves as a common market for almost all Italians. Because of that Passing is well populated and its shops overflow with goods. In the deep of night, the commander brought the fleet to the shore in the vicinity of the settlement. The soldiers and the galleys' fighting contingents disembarked, accompanied by not a small number of hired allies. Under the command of the captain of the commander's galley and arranged in position, they rushed to the settlement. Terrified by the unexpected assault of our troops, the residents fled to the nearby mountain. Our people entered the village and found it vacated by its inhabitants but chockfull of commodities for sale: silk cloths, embroidered woolens called *giambelotti*,[14] colorful carpets and other precious wares. They looted it and took the booty to the galleys; whatever was not worth taking away they burned, setting it to fire.

[1472]

AFTER THUS ENRICHING HIS FLEET, the commander gave orders to return to Modon for winter quarters. For it was already winter, and the harshest season of the year was upon us. But he remained in Modon for only a few days and had to set sail for Lemnos as news came in that the Turkish fleet had moved. It was rumored that the Ottoman had prepared

13. Most likely on the site of modern Çeşme, at the head of the deep bay directly opposite of the city of Chios.
14. High quality Anatolian or Near Eastern woolen or mohair cloth marketed by Italian traders, originally from camel or goat wool, but in the period also from sheep wool, also interwoven or embroidered with silk thread.

✳ THE DEEDS OF COMMANDER PIETRO MOCENIGO

Fig. 6. Modon. From Bernhard von Breydenbach, Peregrinatio in terram sanctam. *Mainz: Erhard Reuwich, 1488.*

forty well-appointed galleys to seize the island. Hearing that, the commander made the necessary arrangements, took provisions on board, and departed with all speed to Lemnos. Once there, he found that the rumor about the Turkish fleet had been false. The island of Lemnos has two castles, called Paleocastro and Cocino.[15] Cocino has been hit hard by an earthquake and was practically destroyed. A good part of the walls and towers of Paleocastro were damaged as well. The commander ordered them restored and renovated with due diligence, placed there a garrison of soldiers he had recruited in the Peloponnese, and setting the affairs of the island in good order, returned to Modon. There he preoccupied himself with the repair and outfitting of his galleys, while in Venice two new legates of the fleet were elected, Stefano Malipiero and Vettor Soranzo, both eminent men well-versed in the city's domestic and foreign affairs.[16]

15. Paleocastro is on the site of modern-day Myrina. I was not able to identify the site of Cocino.

16. Stefano Malipiero, scion of the ancient noble family, was an experienced sailor, and Vettor Soranzo, distinguished naval commander, later served as captain of the sea.

After accepting the charge they went on board a galley and promptly sailed to join the commander. Then, after discussing it, they decided unanimously that each galley should also take on ten horsemen, beside the marines. For from every city in the Peloponnese subject to their dominium or allied with them, the Venetians recruit mercenary riders from the nation of the Epirotes, called in Greek *stratiotoi*.[17] These are courageous men ready for any endeavor. With their frequent depredations, they have devastated the part of the Peloponnese subject to the Ottoman and turned it into a desert. By nature, these people are very rapacious, more prone and better skilled to prey rather than fight pitched battles. They use shields, swords and spears. A few of them wear breastplates; the rest don a kind of corset stuffed with cotton that protects them from the arms of the enemy. Their horses are easy to maintain and are used to long rides. The most valorous among them are from Nauplion, a city of Peloponnese located in the plain of Argolis. Thus, the commander and the legates sailed with the fleet to Nauplion, took the horsemen on board, and with all of their men took off to despoil and devastate the maritime provinces of Asia.

The commander did not wish to inflict even minuscule damage to the islands and provinces of Greece subject to the Ottoman, for apart from their governors and garrisons the majority of the people there are Christian. Asia, however, is a province populated by barbarian and infidel people dedicated and devoted to the superstitious sect of Muhammad. For that reason, sailing around Greece and leaving it behind, the fleet turned to Lesbos. The promontory of that island that extends eastwards is uninhabited and has an excellent harbor; there the squadron put in to port. Across the sea from it sits Aeolia, a wealthy region whose main settlement on the seashore,

---

17. The *stratiotoi* were lightly armed horsemen, mostly Albanians by origin at that time.

Fig. 7. Pergamum. Theater and Palace District. Wikimedia Commons.

called Castro, is located in the plain of Pergamum.[18] In the past Pergamum was a city famous in all Asia. The use of goatskin for writing was invented there, and that is why it is called "parchment."[19] The kings of that city ruled the better part of Asia before the last of them, Attalus Philopator, bequeathed it to the Roman people.[20] Nowadays few vestiges of the city can still be observed, but in its fertile plain there are many villages.

And so, in the deep of night, the horsemen and a good part of the troops disembarked under the command of Jacopo Parisoto, the fleet's master, or as he is called in the vernacular, the admiral. This officer is in charge of piloting and conducting the fleet and judging the sailors and punishing them for minor trespasses, while the grave offenses are under the jurisdiction of the commander. For that reason he was appointed as commanding officer for land incursions. Reserving some horsemen, soldiers, and the galley's crew as a backup force, he

18. Ancient Πέργαμον, now about 26 km. (15 miles) from the Aegean shore, near the modern-day Bergama in Turkey, on the northern bank of the river Caicus.

19. *Pergamentum* or *pergamenum* in Latin.

20. Attalus III Philopator (138–133 BCE).

sent the rest to attack and despoil the area. Splitting into several detachments, the latter sailed forth as eagerly as if released from prison, overran several villages, captured a good deal of men and herds of farm animals, and loaded themselves with a substantial amount of household goods. While our men were returning with the booty, enemy cavalrymen from several places got together, for those who managed to escape from the hands of our men went around hollering and wailing. Now, arraying themselves for battle and issuing a great battle cry, they fell upon our men, hoping to recover the booty. But our horsemen turned their horses and vigorously engaged them. They cut to pieces many and forced the rest to flee. The booty was safely carried to the galleys. The horsemen then brought the heads of the slain enemies to the commander and received a gold piece for each one of them.[21] For he had promised a gold coin for the head of any enemy killed in battle; and this became a custom afterwards.

As soon as the booty was loaded on the galleys, the commander ordered the fleet to a certain island called St. Panagia. Deserted but well provided with harbors, it lies between Chios and the mainland. There the booty was unloaded and three prefects were elected from among the galley captains, two Venetians and one Dalmatian; and the custom of electing officials in this manner was always observed after that. Acting according to the ancient Venetian tradition, the prefects gave a tenth of all booty to the commander. The horsemen kept two thirds of the booty they had seized for themselves, as the commander had promised them, and gave the third part to the prefects. All prisoners of war captured by the marines and the soldiers were consigned to the prefects, who sold them at auction[22] and divided the proceeds as follows. First, to every

21. "Gold piece:" a Venetian ducat.
22. The Ottoman invasion and conquests revitalized significantly the Mediterranean slave market, with abundant supply of Eastern Orthodox,

fighting man who had captured a prisoner were given three gold pieces. Then the galley captains were reimbursed for the expenses incurred to maintain the horses. The rest of the funds were distributed in equal parts to the galleys; the legates of the fleet received double of what went to the other galleys. The galley captains kept a third part of the galleys' share for themselves and divided the rest among the crew and the marines, giving to every man according to his rank.

Once he had expedited these matters, the commander directed the fleet for a night journey to the islands adjacent to Caria, intending to prey on what was once the district of Knidos.[23] Knidos used to be a famous city in Caria, with two harbors and an arsenal. It is now ruined and de-populated, but a few vestiges of its monuments are extant. The building of the theater and the half-destroyed walls of its temples and houses made of square stones can still be seen. Its district is not really farmed and is mostly used for

---

(Greek, Russian, Bulgarian, Serbian), and Caucasian (mostly Circassian and Abhasian) slaves. Muslims entered the market more rarely, mostly as prisoners of war and captives carried off in the manner Cippico describes here. On slavery in the Italian-controlled regions during the period see the old but rich survey of Charles Verlinden, *L'esclavage dans l'Europe médiévale* 2 (Ghent: De Tempel, 1955); more recently Jacques Heers, *Esclaves et domestiques au Moyen-Age dans le monde méditerranéen* (Paris: Fayard, 1996). The Genoese market was more lively and is better studied, see Domenico Gioffrè, *Il mercato degli schiavi a Genova nel secolo XV* (Genoa: Fratelli Bozzi, 1971). There is no good, comprehensive modern study of slavery in late medieval and Renaissance Venice; see for orientation Alberto Tenenti, "Le schiavi di Venezia alla fine de Cinquecento," *Rivista Storica Italiana* 67.1 (1955): 52–69, Charles Verlinden, "Venezia e il commercio degli schiavi provenienti dalle coste orientali del Mediterraneo," in *Venezia e il Levante fino al secolo XV* 1.2, Agostino Pertusi, ed. (Florence: Olschki, 1973), 911–29, and Reinhold Mueller, "Venezia e i primi schiavi neri," *Archivio Veneto*, 5th ser., 148 (1979): 139–42.

23. The ancient Greek settlement of Knidos or Cnidos (Κνίδος), probably a Lacadaemonian colony on the modern day Datsa peninsula in southwestern Turkey.

Fig. 8. Delos, Temple of Apollo. From Victor Duruy, History of Greece. *Boston: Estes and Lauriat, 1890.*

grazing flocks. At the advent of daylight, the commander brought the fleet to a nearby port called Barbanicola.[24] The horsemen and the soldiers disembarked and spread all over the countryside. Encountering no resistance, they captured many people of both sexes and of all ages and as many sheep as they wished but not much else except some carpets and felts. This is because the locals, having no fixed abodes on account of frequently moving with the sheep, built their tents and beds with felt.

Once the booty was loaded on the galleys, the commander ordered the fleet to Delos. This island was once renowned in all of Greece with its famous temple of Apollo and the sacred ceremonies that were performed there but is now deserted and uninhabited. Nonetheless, there are still vestiges extant of the temple and the amphitheater done in white marble and many columns and statues. Among them there is a colossal one, fifteen cubits tall,[25] with an inscription that reads Νάξος

24. Or Papanicola, recorded in portolan maps before 1511.
25. Fifteen cubits equal c. six meters.

Ἀπόλλωνι.²⁶ There are also cisterns of enormous size, still full with water. Here the prefects did the usual division of the booty and the auction at which the captives were sold, and after that the proceeds were distributed according to custom.

When all this was completed, the commander gave the order to return to the city of Peloponnese, for provisions were running low. On the way, in the waters south of the promontory of Maina, he encountered Rechaiense, the leader of the royal fleet, with seventeen galleys. They greeted and acclaimed each other in the manner habitual among mariners and sailed together for Modon. There the commander learned that the cardinal-legate of the pope was arriving with his fleet.²⁷

First stocking up on provisions, the commander and the royal captain set sail together to the islands closest to Asia. Now the knights of Rhodes have a castle which, on account of the military skills and valor of its defendants, is strong and impregnable. It is called Castel di San Pietro and is located in the district of Caria that is opposite to the island of Cos.²⁸ Many Christians who seek to escape servitude to the Turks congregate there from all of Asia every day. Yet because beyond the walls is enemy territory, those in the stronghold are not able to go out even to collect wood.

But listen to the marvelous sagacity and shrewdness of their dogs. Those in the castle keep about fifty dogs, which they send

26. The correct spelling of the inscription is after Choiseul de Gouffier, who saw it in 1776 and transcribed it in his *Discors preliminaire du voyage pittoresque de la Grèce* (Paris: L'Impremerie de la Société Littéraire-typographique, 1783), 61.

27. The cardinal-legate was Oliviero Carafa of Naples, a learned man better known for literary exploits than military achievements. On the operations of his squadron, see Alberto Giglielmotti, *Storia della marina pontifica* 2 (Rome: Tipografia Vaticana, 1886), 342–72.

28. The castle of Bodrum, built by the Hospitallers in 1402, now in the city of Bodrum in southwestern Turkey.

out every night. If they come across a Christian, they approach him benignly and joyfully lead him to the castle. But if the dogs meet an infidel, they go after him barking and tear him to pieces. Some may find this incredible: let them read Pliny's *Natural History*, where he has written even more astonishing things about these animals.[29]

Considering the situation, the commander decided to despoil the villages round about in order to make it possible for those in the castle to go out far enough to obtain what they needed. Consequently, he sailed all night long and before dawn reached the shore close to the castle. At that point, however, he realized that only a small part of the squadron was following him and decided to refrain from action until daybreak. There was no moon that night. It was pitch dark, land ridges impeded visibility, and the pilots led the fleet by mistake to the opposite side of a certain promontory. But in the light of dawn the captains figured that the commander was not with them, pulled on the ropes, weighed anchors, rounded the promontory and promptly joined the commander. As it was already the first hour of the day, he immediately ordered the cavalry and some of the foot soldiers to disembark.

Seeing the fleet, the locals sent all those unfit to fight to flee to the mountain and prepared for battle, relying on their numbers and on the broken terrain. These men are used to constant skirmishes with those in the castle and are among the most valiant in all of Asia. Our troops, perceiving the audacity of the enemy, proceeded in an orderly fashion. As soon as they got as close as a stone throw both sides shouted a deafening battle cry and hurled themselves upon one another. The battle was brutal. Because of the stony terrain, the cavalry was not of much use. The infantrymen and the allies shot at the enemy

---

29. Pliny, *Natural History*, VIII.61: "The qualities of the dog; Examples of its attachment to its master; Nations which had kept dogs for the purposes of war."

from afar with arquebuses and arrows and engaged them with swords and piques at close quarters. The enemy shot arrows, with which they were quite skillful, and badly wounded many of our soldiers. For a long time the outcome was undecided. Then our men, prevailing in numbers and valor, cut many of the enemy to pieces and forced the rest to flee. Several of them were captured alive; others found refuge in the steep mountains and unapproachable gorges.

After they routed the enemy, our men overran the villages and devastated them all, putting them to the sword and fire. Despoiling everything, they returned to the galleys with a good load of carpets. For the women of these parts excel at weaving carpets, and their products are not just for their own use but for sale on the market as well. The captives were few and mostly women who, burdened with belongings they wished to take with themselves, did not manage to escape. Countless enemy heads were brought to the commander; many combatants were also captured alive during the battle. None of ours were killed, but fifty have been wounded by arrows.

Four days later, early in the morning, the fleet arrived at a place in Caria called Tabia in our days. Here the sea surrounds a large part of Caria from two sides and turns it into a peninsula.[30] That used to be the district of Halicarnassus, the capital city of the rulers of Caria. Here Queen Artemisia[31] erected the funeral monument of her husband Mausolus, a building of remarkable size and marvelous appearance, which was called Mausoleum after her husband, and later became one of the Seven Wonders of the World. This is the reason why now all sumptuous funeral monuments are called "mausoleums." We saw the mausoleum's remnants

30. The modern peninsula of Bodrum.
31. Artemisia II of Caria (r.353–351 BCE) was the sister and wife of Mausolus, who ruled after him and built the monumental tomb of her husband.

Fig. 9. The Tomb of Mausoleus, Halicarnassus. Engraving by Philips Galle after Maerten van Heemskerck, Seven Wonders of the World, 1572.

among the ruins of the city. The men in this place are quite negligent. They despise agricultural labor and practice pastoralism. Consequently, our horsemen and infantry fanned out around the countryside, penetrated everywhere, seized a great number of people and animals and without delay brought the booty to the galleys. As soon as everything was onboard, the commander ordered a fleet to an uninhabited island called Capraria.[32] There new prefects were elected for the custom was that the commander designated new officials every time the booty was divided. They distributed the spoils in the usual manner, sold the captives at auction and divided the proceeds among the men.

While these things had been taking place, news came that the papal legate had arrived with his squadron. The commander

32. Capraria, "island of the goats;" there are islands with that name northeast of Corsica, and south of Majorca in the Balearics. I was not able to identify an island with that name in the region described by Cippico.

ordered the ships decked out with arms and crests and sailed out to meet him. The encounter was celebrated with the acclamation of the entire fleet and with festive expressions of heartfelt joy at the arrival of the legate. The commander went to see the legate and saluted him. "You have perhaps heard," he said, "or read, excellent Father, of all those valorous and magnificent deeds that the Senate of Venice has accomplished for the Christian faith and for the freedom of the Church. Now you can see them for yourself. Nine years have already passed since the Venetians, without assistance from any of the Christian princes with the exception of King Ferdinand, keep up and endure such a severe and dangerous war.[33] We spare neither effort nor expense on behalf of the Christian community. In the past few days I have despoiled Aeolia and Caria, rich provinces of the barbarian enemy, of men and animals, and burned them down and put everything to the sword. Now that you are here, we will proceed under your leadership and command." The cardinal responded: "I have read and heard of it, my lord Commander, and now I see with my own eyes that the Venetians have surpassed all kings and princes in their zeal to defend the Christian religion. With arms in hand, the Venetians have defended many Christian provinces and peoples from the rage of the barbarian. And you yourself have excelled above any other general with your remarkable deeds. Your valor has diminished the audacity of the crazed enemy. Proceed, therefore, courageously to pursue your designs. As for myself (since I am a churchman), I will pray to the great and majestic God to grant you fortuitous success. The forces I have brought will be placed under your command." The leader of the royal fleet came to see them as well and joined them with his squadron.

After consulting, they departed for Samos, there to decide how to proceed. The island of Samos is uninhabited, although

33. The reference is to the sixteen-year war between Venice and the Ottomans, 1463–79.

it was once renowned for its fertility. Nowadays it abounds in animals of all kinds and is rich in wild honey, which is found in all of its forests; it is bathed as well with the sweet-tasting water of streams running all over the island. The horsemen and the soldiers disembarked here to rest and refresh themselves. The soldiers and other fighting men went hunting in the forests and places with animal hideouts. And while they were engaged in capturing all kinds of beasts, a young man of Dalmatian origin and language came across a bear of enormous size. He attempted to spear it with his pique, but the bear evaded the blow, grabbed the youngster and threw him on the ground. The youngster, with calm presence of the mind, took hold of the animal's ears with both hands and kept the head of the beast away from his face to avoid being lacerated by its teeth until another youngster of the same nation came behind it and killed it with his sword. A great number of animals were killed all over the place and the fleet was replenished with game. These were days of feasting. The men indulged in eating and drinking. Above all did the Illyrians, who were the most numerous among the marines. Gulping from large cups and singing, they invited their comrades to drink more.[34] And after they ate to satiety they began reminiscing, everyone boasting of their great exploits, for it is customary for idling men to glorify themselves and their victories.

While all this was going on the fleets' leaders gathered together to determine the course of action. The consensus was that they should attack Attalia, a city in Pamphylia founded by Attalus Philadelphus,[35] with appropriate siege equipment. They hoped that if the assault were carried out swiftly and

34. By "Illyrians" Cippico means people of Slavic origin, likely Croatians from the interior.
35. Modern Antalya (also Satalia or Adalia). The city was the chief port of Pamphylia, founded by Attalus II, king of Pergamum (159–138 BCE). In ancient geography, Pamphylia was the region in the south of Asia

by surprise, the city would fall without need of artillery and
breaching the walls. Attalia is the chief coastal city of the entire
province of Asia. Its port is defended on both sides by numerous towers and is closed down with a chain. Syrian and
Egyptian merchants congregate there, and it is the common
market for the whole province. Consequently, the commander
called all galley captains and ordered that every ship construct
two or three ladders and wickerwork.

After all that was needed was promptly prepared, he departed
from Samos. Under a westerly wind he left Rhodes behind
and directed the fleet with all speed toward the islands of
Chelidonia.[36] The knights of Rhodes sent two galleys to help.
The fleet thus numbered eighty-five galleys. Of these, the pope
had provided eighteen, the king seventeen, the Rhodians two,
and the Venetians forty-seven ships, of which twelve were from
Dalmatia. Some of the Venetian galleys were away, charged by
the commander to attend to other tasks.

Once he had determined the number of vessels at his disposal,
the commander moved against the city, which was at a distance
of sixty thousand paces.[37] It was already past the tenth hour of
the day.[38] Fighting an adverse wind throughout the night, the
fleet came to shore close to the city on the third hour of the
following day. He then commanded Vettor Soranzo, one of the
legates of the fleet, to assault the port of the city with ten galleys. Stefano Malipiero, the other legate, was ordered to attack

---

Minor, between Lycia and Cilicia, extending from the Mediterranean
to Mount Taurus (modern day Antalya province, Turkey).

36. A string of islands off the coast, Greek Χελιδωνία, modern Gelidonia,
near Finike, Turkey.

37. Cippico is most likely using the classical Roman *passus*, equal to 5
pes or a length of 4.854 ft. (1.48 m.). The distance to the city therefore
would have been c.89 km. or 48 nautical mi.

38. Late afternoon, or around 4:00 PM, given the season and the count-
ing of the Venetian hours from sunrise.

the city by land with the remainder of the soldiers. The horsemen were sent to occupy the hill above the city and be ready. He exhorted everyone to remember their pristine virtues and combat the vile and deprived barbarian enemy for the benefit of the Christian religion and the greater glory of the Venetian empire, and he pointed out to them that the city was overflowing with gold, silver, and precious items. If they managed to take it, they would be returning home rich men one and all. The men greeted the speech of the commander with cheers. After giving his orders, he stayed on his galley accompanied by the papal legate and the commander of the royal fleet, prepared to intervene as needed.

The cavalrymen quickly overran the country, seized a large number of people and animals, and took position on the designated hill as ordered. Propelled mightily by her oarsmen, Vettor Soranzo's galley sped up toward the port. Bombarded from both sides with artillery shots, spears, and arrows, the ship rammed the chain, broke through it, and entered the port. The rest of his squadron followed. Our men cut to pieces the defendants of the towers round about the port and occupied the towers. Above the port, outside the city walls, there was a well-built fortification, where many merchants resided, for it was a convenient site to load and unload merchandise on board ship. Surprised and much frightened by the unexpected assault of the fleet, they left everything behind and fled into the city. Their warehouses were chockfull with black pepper, cinnamon, cloves, incense, carpets and sundry other merchandise. Our men disembarked, quickly sacked all that, carried the booty to the galleys and then tossed fire into the buildings and burned everything down. Because of the height of the walls there was little hope of taking the city by scaling them and they tried to dig underneath the walls. The captain of the Rhodian detachment approached the city gates with his troops and attempted to force open the locked door with hoes and axes. At the same time, the city defenders walled up the gate from within and wounded our men by throwing darts, other missiles and very heavy stones from the walls. The Rhodian captain was hit by a stone while directing the works and was killed; his troops at once carried the body to the galleys. The wind carried the flames of the burning structures in the way of our men and impeded the assault.

In the meantime Stefano Malipiero surrounded the city from the land side and moved his troops up to the walls. On that side the city was protected by two sets of walls and trenches. Our men pulled up the ladders and quickly scaled the first wall, killing the defenders. But the ladders barely measured up to half the height of the second wall. Despairing of being able to enter the city by mounting the wall, our men brought large beams, leaned them on their sides and covered them on top with wickerwork. Thus prepared, they went underneath and began to dig. They also brought wood, torches of pine wood, and other dry material to the western gate of the city, set it on fire and burned down the wooden doors of the gate. But those inside had fortified the gate with a strong wall. Running up to the walls above, they hurled rocks and other heavy objects at those outside who were digging under the walls. They also poured burning sulfur and oil to set on fire the wickerwork that protected our men from the stones they threw. To clear the walls from defenders our troops shot with bombards and arrows and wounded and killed many of them. The defenders shot back with bombards and other missiles. Not a few of our men fell here. The battle raged unabated on all sides. The legate rode around and exhorted and urged the men to fight vigorously. For their part, the galley captains strove manfully and promptly executed the work that was expected from them.

There was in the city a Christian woman of the Illyrian nation, who had spent many years there in slavery. Running back and forth on top of the walls, she noticed that our men had lost impetus and slowed down their attack, and she began to incite and goad them, saying, "Why are you holding back, men? Are you so fainthearted and slothful to abandon the seizure of this wealthy city, packed with all kinds of barbarian merchandise, and poorly defended? I assure you that the better part of the defenders have already been killed by your arms." Hearing her utter these words, a barbarian approached to seize and whip her. However, oblivious to the danger and ready to face whatever fate had in store for her, she gathered her skirts and threw herself down from the walls. Our men picked her up from the ground half-dead. Commending her soul to Christ, she expired in their hands. Courageous woman! Death saved her from the slavery that she was unable to escape in life. Our men buried her body afterwards.

And so the battle went on until nightfall put a halt to it, our men striving valorously, motivated by glory and greed, while the enemy resisted bitterly and fought for their country, freedom, wives and children. The legates returned to the fleet, leaving before the city a detachment sufficient to prevent anyone from getting in or coming out. The leaders gathered together, and the legates reported on the situation. The city was surrounded by strong, high walls, which were adequately manned by their defenders, and without artillery that would breach the walls there was no hope of seizing it. To bring over artillery from the Peloponnese would take many days. But winter was already approaching and the fleet would not be able to stay safely in port, for the coast of Pamphylia lacks ports. The only port was that of the city, with a capacity of no more than fifteen galleys. Furthermore, the gulf of Pamphylia is quite open and exposed to the winds, above all to the southeasterly and the southerly, which tended to become especially furious in the sea of Pamphylia. Therefore, they all agreed to despoil the territory round about the city on the following day and then lift the siege. Some of the boroughs around the city were full with magnificent houses and with their many splendid villas gave the appearance of real towns. Their orchards were bathed by the waters of clear springs and abounded in excellent fruit-bearing trees. On the following day our men set fire to the houses and burned them down, then cut down the trees and subjected everything else to devastation.

After all this had been quickly carried out, the commander set sail for Rhodes and in a few days arrived there. While in Rhodes, an ambassador arrived from Uzun Hasan, the king of the Persians.[39] He informed the commander, the cardinal and the other leaders of the fleet that the Persian king, persuaded and encouraged by Catarino Zeno, a patrician and an ambassador of Venice, had moved against the Ottoman.[40] His generals and the best of their troops had audaciously invaded Little Armenia, which is subject to the Ottoman, and had seized Tocat, one of the province's strongest fortresses, and several other fortified settlements. He reported that Persia abounds

39. Uzun Hasan (1423–78), the leader of the Turcoman tribal confederation of the White Sheep in eastern Anatolia, cobbled together a large imperial polity in the third quarter of the fifteenth century, comprising Cappadocia, Cilicia, Little Armenia, Kurdistan, Azerbaijan and the better part of modern Iraq and western Iran, with a capital of Tabriz, and was one of the Ottomans' major adversaries of the time. The Venetians first contacted him in 1463, when Lazzaro Querini was dispatched to persuade him to join the war with Mehmet II, but Uzun Hasan waited until 1471 to get involved. On his relations with Venice see the documents in Cornet, ed., *Le guerre dei Veneti nell'Asia 1470–1474*, passim.

40. Catarino Zeno was sent by the Senate in 1471 because he was related to Uzun Hasan via his marriage to Violante, daughter of Niccolo Crespo, duke of the Archipelago. She, in turn, was a sister of the wife of Uzun Hasan. A record of his exploits under the name of *Commentarii* was compiled by his grand-nephew Niccolo Zeno and printed in Venice in 1558, later reproduced several times in the *Viaggi* of Ramusio. Doge Foscarini's antiquarian study of Zeno, *Catarino Zeno: Storia curiosa delle sue avventure in Persia, tratta da antico originale manuscritto, ed ora per la prima volta publicata* (Venice: Vincenzo Formaleoni, 1783), is an extract of Niccolo Zeno's *Commentarii*.

in skillful cavalrymen as well as troops excelling in combat with lances, arrows and swords, but there were none expert or well-versed in other war equipment and armaments. That is why he was sent to the Roman pope, to Venice and to other Christian princes, to ask them to assist his king with the artillery necessary to take cities and harass the enemy from afar. The cardinal, the commander and the other leaders listened sympathetically to the plea of the ambassador and gave him hope that he would achieve his objective. They also gave him a tour of the powerful fleet they led, its ships brimming with the best men and arms one could wish for, and assured him that at a mere nod of his king, it could sail anywhere it was needed.

After seeing off the ambassador, they focused on the tasks at hand while the weather was still favorable. On the western side of Castel San Pietro, which was mentioned earlier, there lays Termerio, a promontory of Myndi, which projects many thousand paces into the sea toward the island of Cos.[41] This is a pleasant province, open to the winds from all sides, with well cultivated olive groves and vineyards, overgrown with a variety of other fruit-bearing trees, and densely populated. Only the men had remained in the area to gather the harvest that autumn. Frightened by the war and the excursions that had recently taken place in nearby regions, they had taken their women and children farther inland. Arriving there, the commander disembarked troops on both sides of the promontory. They ravaged and sacked the country, putting everything whatsoever to fire and sword. The heads of a hundred and thirty-seven enemies who resisted and were cut down were brought to the commander there; many others were captured. The latter were promptly sold at auction, and the proceeds were divided in the usual manner. The soldiers of the pope[42] and the king [of Naples] also got their share.

41. Ancient Myndus, on the far eastern shore of the Bodrum peninsula.
42. Fifteenth-century popes frequently owned slaves, and papal galleys were often rowed by Muslim slaves, mostly prisoners of war, but as the century wore on, the popes became increasingly opposed to

Following this, the commander departed with the entire fleet for the island of Naxos, where he had ordered the supply ships loaded with biscuit to await the squadron.[43] It was already late autumn, and the captain of the royal fleet was given permission to return home with his fleet. The papal legate and the commander discussed whether they still had time to accomplish another worthy endeavor before winter came. The commander had learned that Smyrna, a wealthy city in Ionia, was not well protected.[44] A great portion of its walls had aged and decayed. The inhabitants, used to a long peace, had neglected to repair them. And since the city lay at the head of a long gulf, quite far from busy navigation lines, it was not aware of the war. Its citizens felt secure and lived without fear. Therefore the commander departed from Naxos and set sail for Psyra, an uninhabited island with ruins of an ancient settlement. From there, traveling through the night until the light of dawn, at the third hour of the day he arrived before Smyrna.

Part of the city is built on a mountainside and the larger portion in the plain below it, but the mountainous area is more densely populated. Our men quickly disembarked and surrounded the city from all sides. As many scaled the walls, others made their way through the ruins (for, as it was noted, the walls had fallen apart in many places) and penetrated into the city. The Smyrnians, shocked and frightened by the sudden and unexpected evil, were at a loss as to what to do. Some grabbed their arms and rushed to the ruins to engage the enemy in fighting,

---

enslavement and recommended baptism and emancipation of non-Christian slaves. For this ambiguous attitude during the period see John Francis Maxwell, *Slavery and the Catholic Church: The History of Catholic Teaching Concerning the Moral Legitimacy of the Institution of Slavery* (Chichester: Barry Rose, 1975), 49–52.

43. Naxos was the capital island of the duchy of the Archipelago, and nominally under Venetian suzerainty. The duke, then Giacomo III (1463–80) was under obligation to provide Venetian fleets with assistance.

44. Modern Izmir, in western Turkey.

BOOK ONE *

Fig. 10. Smyrna. From Mark Twain, Innocents Abroad. *Hartford, CT: American Publishing Co., 1869.*

but our men, superior in numbers and valor, cut them to pieces. Others climbed on the rooftops and hurled tiles and stones at our people. Terrified women and maidens sought refuge in the temples, which they call mosques. With disheveled hair, they embraced the altars[45] and prayed to their prophet. Many locked themselves up with their little children in their houses.

Once they had taken the city, our men spread all over the place and ransacked it thoroughly. Some tore the sons from the arms of their mothers, taking the mothers captive as well. Others hauled out of the temples a multitude of women while they kept invoking their prophet Muhammad, dragging by the hairs those who resisted. A widow, passing by the tomb of her husband, embraced it as if it were alive, and prayed for succor,

45. Cippico is either using a trope, since there are no altars in mosques, or referring to the *minbar*, the raised platform in the front area of the mosque, from which sermons, prayer calls and speeches are made.

31

saying "Behold! Will the barbarian enemy separate us whom no power was able to separate in life?" And she would not let herself be moved from there until a soldier pulled out his sword as she gladly extended her neck and cut off her head, retorting "Now you can join your husband!" Many of our men weren't interested in prisoners; instead, they turned to looting houses and seized and carried away precious female ornaments, colorful vestments of different make, copper vases worked splendidly in the Damascene fashion with designs inlaid in gold and silver and other luxurious household items. Wails and laments were heard from all sides. The city overflowed with tears and cries.

Meanwhile, some managed to flee and alerted the city governor, whom these people call *subashi*, that the city has been taken and sacked. He had been at the time in his country house. Balaban (that was his name) quickly gathered together from the nearby places a large force of horsemen and foot soldiers and hastened to assist the city. But the admiral of our fleet, who with a sizable detachment of cavalry and marines was outside the city, ready to repulse attacks, saw the advancing enemy and moved against them. As they came close both sides called out loud, loosened the bridles of their horses, lowered their lances and clashed with one another. The infantrymen followed, joining in the brutal encounter. Instructed by their commanding officers, our soldiers intermixed with the cavalry and wounded the enemies in the face with their long lances. For a while the battle was inconclusive. But as the enemy began to press harder, one of our most valiant and renowned horsemen, Pietro Frasina, pierced with his lance the neck of the enemy leader Balaban, unhorsed him, and despite his resistance cut off his head. A bloody melee ensued. Many of the enemies were cut down, and they turned to flight.

After vanquishing the enemy the victors cut off the heads of the dead and joyously returned to the city. Then they sacked it thoroughly and put it to fire, burning down all houses and other buildings. And so this ancient city, noted for its varied fortunes and many monuments, was reduced to ashes in a few hours. Here I saw many ancient tombs beautifully constructed of square stones and marble. Not a few were ruined, but others still stood up. Among the latter was the memorial of Homer, with a statue and an inscription in Greek letters. The fields around the city are well cultivated, abundantly irrigated by the Melo River, and dotted by several country villas. All these were destroyed by our men, put to the sword and burned down. Two hundred and fifteen enemy heads were brought in and a countless number of captives as well. The booty was loaded on the galleys, and the commander set sail to some islands, which were once inhabited and are now deserted but have their ancient cisterns still full with water. The captives were taken out and sold at auction. The rest of the booty was distributed among the soldiers according to the method that the commander has been using in all raids. The officials then divided the money in the usual manner.

Four days later the commander brought the squadron to the shores of the province of Clazomenae, to a place now called Cape Stilari.[46] Clazomenae was a fortress that lay at the head of the gulf of Smyrna. It is famous for one of its citizens, Anaxagoras, who was the teacher of the philosopher Archelaus and the poet Euripides. The inhabitants of the area, frightened by the example of the ravage of Smyrna, had fled to the mountains and the hinterland. The few that had remained in their homes were captured by our men. Many camels and other livestock were also abducted.

After all this had been carried out, the commander set course for the Peloponnese since winter weather was around the corner. Sailing under a good easterly and accompanied by the papal legate, in a few days he arrived at Modon. It was already winter,

46. Greek Κλαζομεναί, ancient Greek city on the site of modern Urla, on the southern coast of the gulf of Izmir, about 20 miles west of Izmir.

and the papal legate wanted to return to Rome. At his departure, he embraced and kissed the commander. "Illustrious commander," he said, "you have now a solid proof of your virtue. When I apprise the pope and the rest of the Italian princes of your valorous deeds, they will listen in astonishment and admiration. Continue, courageous man, that which you have begun: your glory will be immortal." The commander pledged that he hoped to accomplish even more if only the Christian princes would help the Venetians finish the war with their forces. This said, they parted ways. The cardinal left Modon for Italy; the commander took the fleet to Nauplion to secure the city.

*

Fig. 11. Turkish fortifications on the Dardanelles. From Giovanni Francesco Camocio, Dardanelo fortezza dala parte dela Grecia.... From Isole famose, porti, fortezze, e terre maritime. Venice: Alla libraria del segno di S. Marco, 1572.

BOOK TWO

[1473]

WHILE THE COMMANDER attended to the work on the fortifications a certain Antonio came to see him, a Sicilian youth of great audacity, virtuous and courageous, determined to accomplish a memorable feat. He told the commander that he had been captured at Chalcis by the Turks and then spent a long time as a slave in Gallipoli. There he noticed that the naval arsenal of the Ottoman in Gallipoli was not guarded at night. Also, there was a large warehouse in the arsenal, stockpiled with all kinds of naval equipment such as sails, hemp ropes and other necessities for rigging vessels, sufficient to outfit superbly over a hundred galleys. He told the commander that he was ready to burn down the warehouse together with the fleet, provided he was given what he needed to accomplish this. He requested a fishing boat manned by six companions with whom he would pass through the straights of the Hellespont called the Dardanelles pretending to be a merchant. For in the place where the Hellespont is narrowest the Ottoman had constructed on the two shores two very strong fortresses opposite one another[1] and had mounted on them many guns of incredible size. The fortresses' commanders were under orders to bombard and sink any boat that tried to pass through without permission. The commander praised the youth, promised him much if he carried out what he had conceived and promptly granted his requests.

---

1. The two strongholds, Kale Sultanieh (The Sultan's Fortress) or Çanakkale as it is popularly known, on the Asian side and Kilitbahir (Key of the Sea), on the European side, about twenty-five miles south of Gallipoli, were built in 1463 and later enlarged. Their fortifications are well preserved and Çanakkale is still an active Turkish naval base.

Thus prepared, a few days afterwards Antonio passed through the defenses of the Hellespont and reached Gallipoli on the same day, disguised as a merchant who offered for sale a cargo of apples. He had loaded the boat with the latter to pass for a merchant and conceal the implements he needed to accomplish his task. After nightfall, during the second watch, he sneaked to the warehouse, which he was familiar with and knew well, broke the lock chains with a set of pliers, went inside, and set fire to several corners of the place. And because among other things there were there large quantities of pitch and tallow, the fire surged at once, engulfed everything in no time, and its flames burst outside of the building. While Antonio sped to the arsenal to set fire to the boats the locals, awoken by the roar of the conflagration, gathered from all sides. Alarmed by the multitude and by the shouts of the people who rushed to the blaze, Antonio gave up on the arsenal, hurried to his boat and attempted to sail out of the Hellespont. But as he set out for the opposite shore, the torch that he had hastily tossed in the boat ignited some sulfuric powder laying there and the vessel was engulfed in flames. The boat sank and Antonio and his comrades got to the shore and hid themselves in a nearby forest. Meanwhile the warehouse and everything inside of it burned to the ground.

On the next day the *subashi* of the city ordered a thorough search for the perpetrator of the arson and offered huge rewards for delivering him. A search party came across the apples floating on the water and then sighted the sunken boat; they concluded that the merchant who was selling the apples the day before must have done it. An armed posse was sent to pursue him. They discovered his tracks, which made a trail on the sandy ground, and quickly led them to the forest. As they neared the place where Antonio hid, one of his comrades, a courageous young man by the name of Rado, a Dalmatian from the district of Budua,² desiring to die valiantly, leaped out and hurled himself on the enemy with a sword in his hand and cut down two of them; then arrows and stones from all sides felled him. Antonio and the rest of his comrades were captured alive and led to the *subashi* in chains. The *subashi*, considering that it was not in his purview to put to death the perpetrator of such a deed, sent Antonio and his companions to his prince the Ottoman. As he was brought before the latter, the Ottoman asked him how had he wronged him, or how had his enemies rewarded him, to make his mind to do such a wicked deed to him. But Antonio was undaunted: "As if you don't know that decent men should on principle be fighting you, the common pest of all peoples! You, who have robbed your princely neighbors of their paternal inheritances without any reason; you, perfidious man, who never keeps promises to those who give themselves to you; you, who are never satiated by the blood of your own; you, finally, who strive to extirpate the name of Christians, who are the only people who adore the true God. That is what, I admit, inspired me to do what I did; I wish that I could to do the same to you!" Amazed at the audacity of the youth, the Ottoman ordered him executed together with his companions. They were immediately taken away and cut down through the middle. This is how the valiant young man perished, eager to accomplish a feat beyond his powers. The Venetian senate, unable to reward Antonio according to his merits, compensated his younger brother and his virgin sister. His brother received a yearly stipend and his sister was granted a dowry from the public funds.³

2. A city on the southern Dalmatian coast, located between Bar and Herceg Novi.
3. Cippico models the encounter between Mehmet II and Antonio on the classical story of the Roman hero Gaius Mucius Scaevola who attempted to assassinate the Clusian King Lars Porsena in 508 BCE, as the latter had Rome under siege. Marco Antonio Sabellico, who

In the meantime, while the commander worked through the winter season to fortify the city of Nauplion and have the ships refitted, an envoy came to him with letters from the king of Persia with the same message as the one who had come before him. The commander interviewed him and sent him on a galley to Venice. Prompted by the [Persian] king's envoy and the letters of Catarino Zeno, their own ambassador to the king, the Venetians prepared a great number of guns of various sizes. They also made ready for the king of Persia tableware consisting of engraved gold and silver vases worked in the finest Parisian fashion, many bolts of the finest quality woolens and many vermilion silk clothes embroidered with gold, intended for his personal use. Furthermore, they selected a hundred young men to handle the guns. Their captain was Tommaso of Imola, a city in Flaminia which in antiquity was called the Forum of Cornelius. Then they appointed as envoy Giosafat Barbaro, a patrician of mature age who knew the Persian language well, to deliver all this to the king.[4]

When everything was ready, it was loaded on three large galleys which, even though they are propelled by oars, are better called merchantmen than warships. The Venetians have many galleys of this kind and on them they carry merchandise to all the provinces of the world every year. Thus prepared, the envoy left Venice for Cyprus. From there he could conveniently convey the presents whenever Uzun Hasan would happen to come to the maritime provinces of Cilicia or Syria. It was

---

faithfully follows Cippico, directly referred to the story in his *Historiae rerum Venetarum*, in *Degl' istorici delle cose Veneziane i qualli hanno scritto per pubblico decreto. Tomo primo, che comprende le istorie veneziane latinamente scritte da Marcantonio Coccio Sabellico* (Venice: Lovisa, 1718), 736.

4. Giosafat Barbaro (1413–94), a Venetian merchant, travel writer and diplomat, had already traveled in the region. See *Travels to Tana and Persia and a Narrative of Italian Travels in Persia in the 15th and 16th Centuries*, (Cambridge: Cambridge University Press, 1873, facs. ed., 2009).

reported that at the advent of summer the king would come to these parts. Also, the Senate ordered the commander to be ready to fulfill Uzun Hasan's commandments and anything the king might bid him do, to the detriment of anything else if need be.

The Ottoman, spurred not only by rumors but also after learning from his spies of the large forces and the planned arrival of the king of the Persians, had decided not to waste any more time but to make ready for war and intercept the enemy. And so, apart from his regular troops, he ordered every seventh household in all the provinces under his rule to provide an armed soldier. In addition, he commanded a large number of horsemen and infantry from allied and vassal princes and recruited numerous mercenary soldiers from all nations. Furthermore, he prepared many thousand wagons to form corrals and mounted two guns on every wagon. Also prepared were an incredible number of artillery pieces of all sizes and countless men skillful at manning them. This done, he transferred all of his troops in Thrace to Asia. He also fortified Constantinople and, leaving there a strong garrison under his younger son, led his army against the enemy. He feared very much that the Venetian fleet would seize the fortifications at the Dardanelles Straights and take over the city.

Learning that the Karamans[5] — friends and allies of the king of Persia whom the Ottoman had deprived of their paternal

5. The principality of the Karamanians comprised the southern shores of Anatolia and extended westwards to modern day Mersin. It was one of the Turcoman *gazi* states that rose on the ruins of Byzantium alongside the Ottomans before it was absorbed by Mehmet II in 1483. The Karaman princelings fought an internecine war in the middle of the fifteenth century, and Pir Ahmed came to power with Mehmet II's support. The alliance fell through, however, as he sought to recover territories ceded to Mehmet, and in 1466 the Ottomans invaded and took over the better part of the Karamanians' principality, forcing Pir

kingdom — were attacking the maritime settlements of Cilicia (and also hearing that the older Karaman brother was one of the few friends of Uzun Hasan), our commander decided to do a favor for the king and recover their kingdom for the Karamans. Leaving behind everything that would be of better use to the Venetians to carry out the war, he took with him the galleys that had been refitted and put in good order during the winter as well as the horsemen and set out for Cilicia via Rhodes, where two Rhodian galleys joined him. From there he sailed for Cyprus, whose king was a friend and an ally. The king of Cyprus gave the commander four galleys captained by Zamperio.

Sailing from Cyprus with the entire fleet, the commander reached the coast of Cilicia in the vicinity of Seleucia,[6] which at the time was under siege by the Karaman, and he brought the squadron into the port now called St. Theodore. In that place there was once a settlement dedicated to Venus; the convenient location makes it a well-frequented pirates' lair. To this day a temple of Venus of marvelous size can be seen on the seashore outside the ruins of the city, exquisitely built of

---

Ahmed and Kasim to flee to Uzun Hasan. During Uzun Hasan's invasion in 1472 Pir Ahmed recaptured his patrimony, but after the battle of Beyşehir in 1473 where Uzun Hasan was routed, the Karamanians lost actual power, and the Ottomans kept their state only formally until 1483.

6. Seleucia was one of the principal cities in Cilicia, founded by Seleucus I Nikator, one of Alexander the Great's successors; it flourished in Roman times as main settlement of Cilicia Trachaea and was briefly the capital of the independent state of Isauria in the early 300s. Corycus, Greek Κώρυκος, today Korku or Korghos, was Seleucia's port in ancient, Roman and Byzantine times and another important city in the Roman province of Cilicia Trachaea. The island fortress and part of the land fortifications of Corycus built by the Byzantines still stand. Sighun or Sequin is ancient Syedra, located about 20 km. southeast of modern Alanya, on the eastern side of the gulf of Antalya.

BOOK TWO ✳

Fig. 12. The Temple of Aphrodite at Aphrodisias. From Charles Fellows, An Account of Discoveries in Lycia. *London: J. Murray, 1841.*

rectangular stones.[7] Here came to the commander envoys of Kasim Beg, the younger of the Karaman brothers, who welcomed the arrival of the commander. (Pir Ahmed, the other princeling of Cilicia, was with the army of the king of Persia.) They added that due to the hereditary friendship with the Venetians, the Karamans had always much counted on their valor. It had been the fourth month already, they explained, since their prince had laid siege to three cities, Sighun, Seleucia and Corycus and, if he could seize them, he would take over the entire kingdom. But he lacked artillery and men experienced in taking over cities. So that Kasim Beg might get back his paternal kingdom, which the Ottoman had occupied by

7. Most likely the site of the ancient Aphrodisias, on a promontory about 50 km. (31 mi.) west of Seleucia, with two convenient harbors on the eastern side, in the direction of Seleucia. It was known as *oppidum Veneris* in Roman times. The early Byzantine name of the settlement was *Portus Cavalerius*. This is the best harbor in the vicinity of Seleucia which would have shielded Mocenigo's squadron.

41

force, they asked the commander to assist him with his arms, for he was an ally to the king and friend to the Venetians. The commander sent the envoys back with good words and promises. Then he dispatched Vettor Soranzo as his envoy to the Karaman to learn about the state of affairs and discuss with him what needed to be done first. Riding fast, Vettor appeared before the Karaman and saluted the prince. "I am sent by the commander," he told him, "to let you know that he has come to assist you with a mighty fleet in the name of the friendship with your father and the king of Persia with whom we are now allied. He wishes you to explain to him the state of affairs and what ought to be done right away so that we can agree to take up what needs immediate attention."

Kasim Beg praised the commander and said, "The Venetian Senate has never failed my expectations, and now I can see well that more than any other people the Venetians assist their friends and allies when they fall on hard times. It has been many months now that I have besieged in vain these Cilician cities, for I have neither the machines necessary to seize them nor valiant soldiers. My entire army, except for a few picked men, is composed of simple soldiers, better used to toiling in the fields than waging war. I badly need your help since I can see that you have many experienced troops and a great number of artillery pieces suitable to battle cities." Then he filled him in on the three cities under siege. Two of them were under Ottoman governors. The third had been taken over by force by Mustapha, a perfidious Cilician, who had once been among his most intimate friends but out of greed had gone over to the Ottoman. Because of this, he asserted, nothing would be better than to seize Sighun, Mustapha's residence. If it were to fall, it would serve as an example to all Cilicians to keep faith.

After hearing the Karaman's position, Soranzo returned to the commander and informed him of what had been discussed.

Then the commander dispatched the galley captain Coriolano Cippico of Trogir[8] to scout the city's site and fortifications and after diligently reconnoitering everything to report back. Coriolano duly surveyed everything and returned to report that the city was about two thousand paces from the sea and was built on a rugged, high hill very steep on the eastern side. Otherwise the walls that surrounded the city were weak and without battlements; the inhabitants were not fit to fight. The city was a natural stronghold but it was not well fortified or defended. It could be taken by assault, he affirmed, or the enemy could be pressured to surrender.

With that information the commander dispatched a captain of the Venetian squadron, Alvise Lombardo, with ten galleys to Corycus with the order to make sure that while he laid siege to Sighun the inhabitants were not supplied with provisions via a sea line; Karamanian troops besieged Corycus on the land side. Then with the rest of the fleet the commander arrived before Sighun, disembarked all troops, and directed the fleet admiral to attempt a surprise attack on the city to see if it could be taken without the use of artillery. The admiral moved the marines against the city and surrounded the walls from all sides, bringing along ladders, wickerwork and other equipment necessary for the siege. Each galley captain led his soldiers to the assault. The inhabitants hurled heavy stones down the steep slopes that killed our men approaching from below; shooting weapons from above, they flung them back from the walls. But the defenders fought without the protection of battlements and parapets and were exposed to hits. Our men wounded and killed many of them by shooting arrows and other missiles with their weapons. After a while the admiral realized that in the absence of artillery that would breach the walls the city could not be seized with ladders and other equipment and

8. This is the first time Cippico mentions himself in the account.

gave the signal to retreat and abandon the siege. The walls were too high and the broken-ground approaches to the ramparts, strewn with rocks, made the assault very difficult. The elated inhabitants, although many of them have been killed, felt like victors and taunted, "Go, Venetians, to rule over the sea and the fishes! The government of the land and its cities belongs to the Ottoman!" The admiral reported to the commander that nothing would be achieved without artillery. If he wanted to take the city, only guns would serve the purpose.

The next day the commander sent a messenger to Mustapha to inform him that he would want to experience the goodwill rather than the arms of the Venetians: he should surrender the city or expect the worst. To this Mustapha replied that he was already familiar with the arms of the Venetians and knew that due to its location and defenses the place was impregnable. He did not fear a long siege either since he had provisions in abundance. Therefore he was willing to neither yield the city nor put himself into the hands of another. Hearing Mustapha's reply, the commander mounted his horse and together with the legates of the fleet rode around the city carefully scrutinizing everything, notwithstanding the arrows and other missiles shot at him from the city. He noticed that on the northern side the ramparts were weaker and the hill less steep and rocky and the assault of the attackers would be easier if the walls could be breached. Considering that, he ordered two guns to be brought up and pointed toward the northern side of the walls. When Mustapha realized that the huge machines were being positioned and everything else prepared for the assault, he was terrified by the unexpected adversity and sent one of his intimates, a man of mature age, to the commander, promising to surrender the city on the condition of safe conduct for himself and all of his people and their belongings, to go wherever they pleased. The commander openly pledged his faith and gave leave to

BOOK TWO ✱

Mustapha to go wherever he wanted, then accepted the surrender of the city and consigned it to Yusuf, a prefect of the Karaman, who was present there.

Fig. 13. Corycus. From Victor Langlois, Voyage dans la Cilicie et dans les montagnes du Taurus exécuté pendant les années 1852–1853. *Paris: B. Duprat, 1861.*

With this accomplished, he sailed with the troops to Corycus. On the way there he was joined by Cencius,[9] appointed by King Ferdinand as his fleet's commander, with ten galleys. Corycus is bounded by the sea on two sides. On the third side, toward the land, it is protected by a deep moat and is surrounded by a double set of ramparts. The port is on the western side, and those wishing to enter it pass close to the city walls. Opposite the southern side, at about three hundred paces from the city, lays the island of Eleusia. It is occupied in its entirety by what was once the palace of King Archesilaus, an ancient edifice beautifully constructed by square blocks of white marble.[10]

9. Cencio Orsini, a seasoned naval commander of the Hospitallers, who later went on to serve the papacy, see Alberto Guglielmotti, *Storia della marina pontifica nel medio evo dall 728 al 1499*, 2 (Vatican City: Tipographia Vaticana, 1886), 384–87, 400–402.

10. Cippico refers here the island fortress of Corycus, built by the Byzantines. "Archesilaus" is most likely a confusion, perhaps with the better-known four kings of Cyrene with that name, who ruled in the fifth century BCE and are mentioned by Herodotus, Pindar and other classical authorities, or with the fourth-century BCE Platonic philosopher Archesilaus, and the person Cippico actually meant, the last king of Cappadocia Archelaus Sisines, or Ἀρχέλαος, a Roman client prince

45

The inhabitants had positioned many guns and other military equipment on top of the walls that faced the port, seeking to block anyone who would have attempted to enter uninvited. As he drew close to the city the commander first surveyed everything in detail and then, mounted prominently on the high stern, directed with his own hand the course of the admiral who led the entry into the port under a steady fire of artillery shots and arrows. The king's commander followed after him, then the legates with all of the fleet. The commander had the troops disembark and then sent a messenger to the governor to admonish him to surrender the city or suffer the fate that victors mete out on the vanquished.

Now it is the custom of the rulers of the Turks to take the fifth part of the prisoners of war captured by their commanders during military expeditions in foreign lands. Above all others they prefer to select ten- to sixteen-year old boys. If there are no captives, they collect the sons of Christians from all Christian provinces of their empire against the will of their parents, turn them away from the Christian faith and the worship of the true God and into the Muslim superstition and give them over for instruction to masters that educate them in all the arts of war. When they grow up, they fight for the ruler and are called Janissaries.[11] Those of superior birth or qualities are promoted to high positions. The army leaders, the provincial governors, and the town and fortress commanders are selected from among them. Of the rest some serve in town garrisons, others as the ruler's personal guard whom he sends to war and into battle and wherever he goes. This contingent is the strongest of the Ottoman army and is practically an invincible

(first century BCE–17 CE). Eleusia is the island of the port town Elaiusa Sebaste, granted to Archelaus by Octavian Augustus in 25 BCE, where he later transferred his palace.

11. On the Janissary corps see Godfrey Goodwin, *The Janissaries* (London: Saqi Book Depot, 1997).

cohort. For the current ruler as well as his predecessor owe all of their military victories to the arms and valor of the Janissaries. To that cohort belonged the city commander Ismael, a man of the Illyrian nation from Lower Pannonia, raised as a Janissary since his early years. The Ottoman had given him a hundred and fifty soldiers to defend the city.

Ismael responded that he was not Mustapha the Cilician, sent to defend a city with a multitude of fearful shepherds and peasants. Rather, he was a commander of the praetorian cohort in charge of a company of Janissaries, valiant men accustomed to gun powder, wounds and blood since adolescence, prepared to suffer extreme hardship to maintain their faith. After he received Ismael's response, the commander went around the city to scout the best places for the artillery. Surveying everything, he decided to position and aim two large guns capable of breaching walls on the western side and to place another one on the island to the south of the city. On the commander's order the admiral diligently attended to the unloading of the guns and everything else necessary for their operation. Above all, the artillery pieces have to be protected so that those who operate the equipment can do it in safety from the gun shots of the enemy.

Hence a couple of days passed until the battle gear and other equipment was moved and placed into position. In the meantime our men constantly engaged the defenders and shot at them with arrows and other missile-throwing weapons. For their part, the defenders tried to impede the work of our men by shooting with guns and arrows. Consequently, not a few of our men and many of the defenders fell wounded. Now everything was prepared for breaching the walls. The gun that shot at the ramparts from the isle had already demolished a good part of the first wall when Ismael, seeing that the segment of the walls on the southern side was in ruins and that two large guns were positioned close to the other side of the walls ready for action, panicked and in exchange for a safe conduct for himself and his troops surrendered the city to the commander. The commander accepted the capitulation of the city, and with all of the military equipment that was found there he handed it over to the Karaman. He ordered that Ismael and his companions be transported to Syria on board our galleys, according to the agreement.

Then he set off for the coast close to Seleucia. Seleucia is an ancient city, built by Seleucus, one of Alexander's successors, five thousand paces from the sea. It used to be a very large city, adorned by splendid neighborhoods and many other monuments. The river Calycadnus ran through it and irrigated the ample fields round about.[12] Many vestiges of buildings are still visible, especially on the river banks. Here we saw, apart from the ruins of temples and the amphitheater, an almost completely preserved square portico which only lacked the roof, richly decorated with columns, statues and other sculptures.[13] It hurt me to see that such an excellent work, produced at great expense, had been ruined due to the neglect of the barbarians.

The current town encompasses only the area of the stronghold of that city.[14] It is situated on a steep-sloped hilltop and is fortified by strong walls of ancient workmanship and a moat. Its captain was Hasim Beg, a Greek by origin, with two hundred Janissaries under him. The commander sent the admiral to reconnoiter the layout of the town and its fortifications and to admonish Hasim Beg to give back the town — which had been taken over by force by the Ottoman — to the Karaman who owned it by fatherly and grandfatherly right. The admiral promptly went to the town and diligently surveyed it. He then

12. Modern Göksu River.
13. See Fig. 14 for these ruins, still to be seen in Seleucia.
14. The late medieval and modern settlement of Taşucu.

Fig. 14. Seleucia. Ruins of Tombs. Wikimedia Commons.

called for Hasim Beg and told him: "You know that Seleucia is no better fortified than Sighun and Corycus and that you are of no higher provenance or nobler virtue than Mustapha, nor are you stronger and more skillful in war than Ismael. They preferred to experience our commander's mercy rather than his might. Following their example, you ought to restore the town to those to whom it belongs by hereditary and natural right. If you do not do it now, while everything is still intact and before the commander brings up the siege artillery and other machinery and prepares everything necessary for capturing the town, you will later have no hope for his mercy."

To this Hasim Beg replied that brave men do not follow the example of others but count on their natural resourcefulness and declared that he would remain faithful to his ruler. The admiral heard the captain's response and went back to the commander. He reported that the town was exceptionally well fortified by natural and man-made defenses and that he had not been able to persuade the captain to surrender. Therefore, if he wanted to seize the town, force was needed, not words. The commander considered Hasim Beg's decision and charged the admiral to prepare for the siege. The admiral took the mandate and diligently applied himself to the commander's directive. He ordered that a fort was built close to the town and that roads were cleared for bringing in the military equipment. As Hasim Beg observed from the town all this taking place, I think he got alarmed that if he waited longer he would be given no quarter were the commander to proceed any further. He sent one of his men to the commander with the following message: "Invincible Commander, cognizant of your clemency through the experience of others, I am surrendering myself and the town to you and would rather have your safe conduct than the Karaman's. Therefore, send an appropriate man to accept the submission of the town."

The commander praised the decision of the captain and sent his legate Vettor Soranzo to carry out the business. Vettor immediately went to the town, accepted its submission from the captain, and transferred it over to the Karaman, who was also there. Then the Karaman, through the work and persuasion of the legate, hired Hasim Beg and his troops to fight for him as mercenaries. Thereafter, as the Karaman saw that his kingdom had been recovered through the effort and courage of our commander, he sent him as a present a horse adorned with a saddle and harness made of silver and a tame leopard for the prosperity and success of his endeavors, together with his thanks for having restored the kingdom to him through force and courage even though he had merited it.

*

WHILE ALL THIS was taking place in Cilicia, due to the remoteness of the region, apart from vague rumors nothing certain had been heard of the army of the king of Persia and the expedition of the Ottoman. Therefore, as there was nothing else to do in Cilicia Trachaea (since all of maritime Cilicia to Mount Taurus was now under the Karaman) and he did not want to waste time, the commander decided to move on Lycia, for that province was still intact. However, he heard that the king of Cyprus was suffering from dysentery and made a diversion to pay him a visit. He found him gravely ill and comforted him to bear the affliction with patience. The king then told him: "You see," he said, "illustrious Commander, that due to the onslaught of this grave illness I have reached the end of my life. I feel that the spirit of life has left me. Therefore, I institute as my heirs my pregnant wife and my posthumous child. She is the daughter of your fellow citizen Marco Corner. The Venetian senate gave her in marriage to me as its adopted daughter. Thus, if the fates take me away, I commend my spouse and my kingdom to the Venetian senate. In the name of our friendship and in the name of the majesty of the Venetian empire, pledge and swear that if death overtakes me you will defend my heirs and my kingdom from harm."[15]

15. James II of Lusignan married Caterina Cornaro, daughter of Marco Cornaro, on July 30, 1468, by proxy in Venice. Since Caterina was 14 years old at the time, she remained in Venice and moved to Cyprus in 1472, when the marriage was officially concluded and the union consummated. James died soon thereafter, and his will appointed Caterina as the kingdom's regent in the name of his posthumous child, the future James III. See David Hunt, Iro Hunt, and Peter Edbury eds., *Caterina Cornaro, Queen of Cyprus* (Nicosia: Trigraph, 1989); and Giuseppe Campolieti, *Caterina Cornaro: Regina di Cipro, Signora di Asolo* (Milan: Camunia, 1987).

The commander urged the king to hope for the best and assured him that being young and strong of body he would easily overcome the illness. However (since the life of mortals is uncertain) if his days were over, he pledged that the senate of Venice and he himself, who was their commander, would protect his heirs in case of danger and defend his kingdom.

Thus lifting the spirits of the king, he took his leave and swiftly sailed with the entire fleet to the islands adjacent to Lycia. He had heard that there was in that province, not far from the coast, a very rich town called Mycra and made his mind to seize it.[16] The town is perched on top of a high, steep ridge located in the middle of a plain that extends all the way to the sea and is surrounded by hills on all sides. Very fertile fields irrigated by the river Lorimo and dotted with numerous villages stretch outside of the plain. And so, early in the morning the commander led the fleet to the shore outside the plain.

The horsemen and the marines disembarked and quickly spread all over the fields. They ransacked and plundered the villages and took a huge amount of booty in captives and other spoils. When that was done, he brought the fleet into the bay closest to town, and all the soldiers went ashore. In charge of the town's defenses was Karadja, a Tribal, with one hundred and fifty Janissaries.[17] The commander sent an envoy to him to admonish him to surrender the town lest the walls were razed to the ground, the town seized and he himself, put in chains, see his people mocked and derided. To this Karadja replied that he was of such origins that he would rather suffer in the extreme than be disloyal.[18] On account of the

---

16. It is not clear if Cippico does not confuse this settlement with ancient Myra in Lycia.

17. "Tribal" or Serbian, another Janissary commander of Slavic origins well known to Cippico.

18. As elsewhere, Cippico uses the classical Roman virtue of *fides* to denote the link between the Janissaries and their master, the Ottoman sultan.

location, the walls and the defenders he held himself unconquerable and declared that he had pledged his faith and would render the town only to his ruler, from whom he had received it.

Receiving this response from the captain, the commander prepared for siege. Since there was only one way through which horsemen could pass into the plain, very narrow and close to the seashore (everything else was closed by a continuous ridge in the shape of a theater) he ordered it sealed by a mound and a moat and placed a detachment to guard the approaches to it so that if the enemy appeared they would not be able to divert our men from the siege and bring succor to the inhabitants. Then he surveyed the area and positioned three large guns against the western side of the town, and a fourth one against its eastern side and ordered the town completely surrounded so that no one could either enter or exit. After quickly preparing all that was needed for the operation of the war machinery, the guns began to batter the walls with frequent shots that damaged and demolished them. Our soldiers attempted to break through into the town and harassed the defenders. Those who broke cover trying to repulse our men got wounded by arrows shot from afar. The citizens incessantly hurled missiles of all kinds to deter and wound our people all over the place, especially those who manned the war equipment. In the meantime Ajas Beg, the *subashi* of the province, had gathered a large force of horsemen and set off to relieve the town. When our horsemen learned that the enemy was approaching, they quickly took hold of their arms, saddled and mounted their horses, and advanced to meet them in battle, arranged in four columns. As they sighted each other, both sides spurred their horses and clashed together. At the first run our men unhorsed many of the enemy. Ajas Beg was killed, pierced by the lance of Peter Bozhich, the captain of our horsemen; the rest took to flight at once. Many enemies were killed, others captured alive, still others sought refuge in the nearby forests and marshes.

Victorious and rejoicing, our men returned to the commander, bringing with them a hundred and fifteen heads of dead enemies and sixty-four captives. The commander ordered the enemy heads stuck on spears and exhibited to the defenders. Two towers were already destroyed by artillery fire and the wall between them was breached. Karadja saw that those who came to succor him had been killed or fled and that there was no longer hope of being rescued, and that the walls had been partially demolished. As the citizens urged him to surrender, he became anxious lest it became too late and sent to the commander offering him the town with everything in it except the free persons. And so, the commander took over the town and gave license to Karadja and all the citizens to go wherever they pleased. The soldiers got the booty and the town was set on fire and razed to the ground. The suburbs around the merchants' square were densely built up with ample houses and the gardens were well irrigated and diligently cultivated; all this was put to the sword and destroyed by fire.

After this was done, the commander set sail and made a landfall at Fiscum. Fiscum used to be a town in Lydia, situated in the province of the city of Rhodes.[19] Nowadays one can barely see its vestiges. Its region, however, is still dotted by villages, all of which our men sacked. But the commander had better accomplishments in mind and decided to pass through the defenses of the Hellespont, desiring to strike a heavier blow at the enemy. To this end he called in the galley captains to advise them of his intentions and ordered them to have the ships ready and on alert.

✳

19. Most likely Physcus, actually in the ancient province of Caria, district of Rhodia Perae, at the promontory at whose head sits Cnidus.

WHILE THE COMMANDER BUSIED HIMSELF with this, two envoys arrived, sent by Charlotte, the sister of the king of Cyprus, who had been exiled from the kingdom by her brother for many years and now resided on Rhodes. She was married to Louis, the son of the duke of Savoy, a sluggard man who had abandoned his spouse at home and led a licentious life with concubines.[20] The envoys informed the commander that the king of Cyprus, who had deprived Charlotte of her hereditary right over the kingdom against the law, had died. Because of that they asked him to help her recover her hereditary kingdom, for she was the daughter of the former king of Cyprus who had been a friend of Venice and was the daughter-in-law of the duke of Savoy, an ally of Venice, and she was born of a legitimate wife while her brother was born of a concubine. To this the commander responded that King James of Cyprus had been a friend and an ally of Venice and had possessed the kingdom legitimately, because kingdoms do not pass under the rule of kings though legal formulas or contested litigation but through arms and bravery. The commander stated that James had not seized the kingdom from his sister but had courageously torn it from the hands of the Genoese, who had tyrannically occupied the better part of the

20. Charlotte Lusignan (1444–87) was the eldest daughter of John II of Lusignan and the Byzantine princess Elena Palaiologina. She succeeded to the kingdom of Cyprus in 1458 after the death of her father and was dethroned by James II in 1463. She was first married to John of Portugal or Coimbra (1431–57), but became widowed in 1457, and then married Louis of Savoy (1437–82), son of Duke Louis I of Savoy (1440–65) on October 4, 1459. After her ousting from Cyprus in 1463, Charlotte went in exile to Rome and then to Rhodes, where she resided with many of her Byzantine Greek relatives. In her bid to keep and recapture the kingdom she was supported by the Genoese, who held Famagusta between 1372 and 1464, hence Mocenigo's retort to her envoys that James II, who enjoyed the support of Venice and above all the Mamluks of Egypt, had torn it out of the hands of the Genoese.

island for a long time, and he had been its lawful ruler thereafter. He declared that now the rightful heir was the queen, the adopted daughter of the Venetian senate, with her posthumous child (for she was pregnant), and that both he and the senate of Venice would defend the queen and the kingdom against anyone who would like to cause them any harm. The envoys received the reply and left displeased.

So arranging everything, the commander prepared to set sail toward the Hellespont when letters from the ambassador Catarino Zeno arrived, through which he informed him that the armies of the king of Persia and the Ottoman, the price of the Turks, were closing on each other and in a few days would clash together determined to resolve their differences through the force of arms. Furthermore, the ambassador advised the commander to sail immediately to Cilicia with the entire squadron, stating that Uzun Hasan himself was certain to arrive there soon to discuss with him everything pertaining to the war. Voyage plans thus changed, the commander directed the fleet toward Cilicia, but as the horsemen had run out of fodder for the horses, he disembarked the troops in what once used to be the plain of Myra.

Myra was a city in Lycia, one of the six cities that were prominent among the Lycian settlements for their size and importance.[21] Many vestiges of the ruined city are still visible, especially funerary monuments cut out from the living rock and adorned with columns and statues sculpted and carved in the same stone. Our men spread about and captured a few people who had remained to guard the villages. But the rest, moved by fear, had fled to impassable crags and mountain ridges. Still, a great quantity of wheat and barley was brought in.

---

21. At the site of modern Kale or Demre in the province of Antalia, Turkey.

After loading the galleys with enough barley to feed the horses for several days, the commander departed and sailed for Cyprus. After arriving in Famagusta, he paid a visit to the queen, who was in mourning on account of the recent demise of the king and lamented him, stricken by heavy sorrow.[22] The commander comforted her, brought up many examples of the fragility of humanity and the unstable vagaries of fortune and with copious words offered his services whenever she needed him. The queen, although she was as afflicted by an incurable wound and could barely raise her face and speak, grieving and suffused in tears as she was, nonetheless lifted her eyes, thanked the commander and with entreating words commended herself and the kingdom to him.

The queen somewhat consoled, the commander left her and sailed for Cilicia, there to wait for Uzun Hasan. While he stayed in the port of Corycus with the armada, Alvise Loredan arrived, a galley captain of the papal fleet. For the pope had sent his legate Lorenzo Zane, archbishop of Split, with ten galleys. But as he reached Rhodes he did not want to proceed any further before first notifying the commander of his commission and his plans.[23] And so Alvise informed the commander that the archbishop, a legate sent by the pope, had arrived at Rhodes and desired to know whether there was anything worthy planned, and if there were, he promised to join in the endeavor. To this the commander replied: "Both last year and this year I successfully accomplished many feats which, given

22. James II died on the night of July 6, 1473. Mocenigo arrived in Famagusta on August 18, but then had to leave on orders of the Senate.
23. Lorenzo Zane (1429–85), archbishop of Split 1452–75, then Latin patriarch of Antioch, obtained the bishopric of Treviso, and finally that of Brescia. He was also a military man and fought for the papacy against the counts of Anguillara, in the siege of Rimini — where he was wounded, in the wars with the Ottomans, in the subjection of Umbria to the pope and in other encounters.

the greatness of his spirit, may seem trifling to the legate, but they have hurt the enemy, and the Christian princes consider them impressive and egregious. If it were not known to all, I would mention that the entire sea coast from the Hellespont to Syria lay prostrated before our arms and our courage, and was all devastated. We have now set our minds to something no less important. It is up to the legate to decide whether to come along. I would be glad to welcome him if he decided to join, both on account of my reverence for the pope to whom respect is due and because of the person of the legate who had spent a long time under arms in the plain of Piceno and is not a novice in the matters of war."[24] With that response Alvise went back to the legate.

After lingering for many days at the coast of Cilicia without news about the progress of the Persian king, the commander finally received letters from Catarino Zeno, which informed him that the army of the Persian king had clashed two times with the Turks. The Ottoman has two high commanders, called the pasha of Anatolia and the pasha of Romania. The first is in charge of all Asian, the second of all European provinces subject to the Ottoman. He relies heavily on their advice in administering the empire and on their effort in waging war. In the first battle the son of the king with thirty thousand horsemen squared with forty thousand led by the pasha of Romania. And as the Persian horsemen were superior by far to the men and horse of the Turks, the Turks, not able to withstand even the first attack of the Persians, turned to flight and were almost all cut to pieces. The pasha himself and several magnates were killed; others were captured alive and led before the king.

---

24. Piceno here means the area of the March of Ancona with Ancona, Termo and Ascoli.

On the next day the king, elated by the prospect of success, surrounded the camp of the Ottoman with all of his troops. It is the custom of the Ottoman to build for himself a private compound in the middle of the camp and to reside there as if in a fortress. In this expedition he had had fortified a place with a mound and a moat about four thousand paces in circumference. All around behind the mound he had placed wagons chained together and on each wagon were mounted two pieces of artillery. Apart from that, a great quantity of guns of all sizes were designated for the defense of the fort. To man all that equipment he assigned fifteen thousand men expert in handling guns and all other kinds of artillery. Within the fort he kept twenty-five thousand horsemen, selected from the entire army. These were mostly Thracians and Tribals.[25] There were also twenty thousand infantry called Janissaries, an invincible battalion similar to the Macedonian phalange.

Now the Persians, after forcing the rest of the Ottoman army to flee, approached the fort. The Ottoman soldiers behind the mound saw them closing on the stronghold and fired all guns simultaneously, causing a miserable slaughter of the enemy. Here the son of the king, an audacious youth who fought ferociously in the first ranks, was killed, shot and transfixed by a cannon ball. Then the rest of the Persians took to flight, horrified by the sight of their men as they saw them falling, some with their limbs torn up, others with their intestines spilled out, and also because they could not control their horses, which were frightened by the terrible thunder of the artillery and unaccustomed to the roar of the guns. The Turks poured out from the fort and fell on those who fled but the soldiers of the king spurred their horses and quickly slipped away to save themselves, for the entire army of the king was on horseback. The

---

25. Serbians and Greeks or Bulgarians from Thrace, according to the toponymy Cippico is using.

Turks broke into the Persian camp and ransacked it thoroughly, neglecting the pursuit of the enemy. Unharmed, the king with the army retreated to the mountainous areas of Armenia, where his wife and children were. The Ottoman, upon seizing the enemy's camp and his military equipment, counted himself the winner, dismissed the army and went back to Byzantium.

In that war there were three hundred and fifty thousand soldiers in the king's army, and three hundred and twenty thousand in the army of the Ottoman. Ten thousand men of the king's and forty thousand of the Ottoman's men perished. The Ottoman triumphed over the king not because of his soldier's numbers or valor but because of his astuteness and his artillery.[26]

All this the commander learned from the letters of Catarino Zeno, and as he advised him not to expect the king this year (for the king had taken the army to winter quarters), he left Cilicia and set off for Cyprus to congratulate the queen on the birth of her son, since he had heard that he had been born, and to see as well whether it was necessary to protect the kingdom.[27] He visited the queen and after paying her his compliments, at her wish, the commander and the legates of the fleet took the baby boy to the baptismal font, and the child was given his father's name. The boy baptized, the commander took his leave from the queen. The queen's uncle Andrea Cornaro was in Cyprus, a man of gentle spirit and benign demeanor, raised since his youth in excellent manners, more prone to suffer than to cause harm. The queen relied much on his advice for the governance of the realm. The commander summoned him and inquired about the affairs of the kingdom and the loyalty of the vassals and whether he feared or needed anything. He replied

26. The battle took place on August 11, 1473, at Otlukbeli and ended Uzun Hasan's engagement of the Ottomans for good. Mocenigo was back in Cyprus on September 26, 1473.
27. James III of Lusignan (August 1473–August 1474).

that everything was calm and secure and assured him that for the moment there was no need of anything. The commander, however, fearing what may come, added two ships to the great galleys that had brought the artillery and the other presents for the king of Persia and left them in Famagusta for defense purposes. The captains were ordered to respond to Cornaro.

Meanwhile the papal legate arrived with two galleys to see the commander and told him that the other eight ships had been taken to Chios by the treasurer sent by the pope to oversee the squadron's expenses. The commander briefed him on the war of the Persian king with the Ottoman. The legate went back with him, and they left Cyprus together. The minds of all were preoccupied with the army of the king of Persia and the outcome of the war. The commander feared that the Ottoman, given his usual shrewdness to depress the spirits of the enemy, would announce how he had defeated the Persian king and forced him to flee (for he would often order festivities and other celebrations of victory even when he had lost). The commander therefore sailed first to Rhodes, then to Chios and to other Greek islands, stating everywhere that even though the king had lost his camp, he had been superior in battle and had killed more enemies and that they should not trust that mendacious enemy the Ottoman. Encouraging them in this way, he sailed past the Sporades and the Cyclades, came to the Peloponnese and docked in Modon because winter had already arrived and because he had received a letter from friends, which informed him that his replacement would soon be appointed. He decided to remain there to wait for the decree of the Senate that would recall him home. The papal legate with the two galleys (we did not see the other eight) and the king's commander with his squadron left Greece and returned to Italy.

*

Fig. 15. Famagusta by Giovanni Francesco Camocio. From Braun and Hogenberg, Civitates Orbis Terrarum I. Cologne: Typis Theodori Graminaei, 1572.

BOOK THREE

[1473]

WHEN KING JAMES OF CYPRUS took over the realm, he demoted some of the nobles and barons of the island who had taken the side of his sister Carlotta, sent others into exile and promoted to the highest positions foreigners of low extraction and men who had practiced piracy. Most of them were from that part of Nearer Spain which is now called Catalonia. Used to living by despoiling others and not content with what was theirs, even though they were in possession of large estates granted them by the king, now that the king was dead they hatched a conspiracy. Among them was the archbishop of Cyprus, who had been sent by his king as an envoy to Ferdinand, the king of Naples.[1] Hearing of the death of the king, he made up his mind to seize by force the kingdom of Cyprus together with his compatriots in whose hands were the fortresses and the magistracies of pretty much the entire island. He figured it would be very expedient for this if a son of the king of Naples born of a concubine wedded a daughter of King James of Cyprus of similar provenance, and with much persuasion he convinced the king to contract the marriage. And so the king sent two galleys to take one of his intimates and the archbishop to Cyprus.

---

1. The leader of the Catalan party, bent on surrendering the island to Ferdinand II of Naples was Louis Perez Fabregues, archbishop of Nicosia and the younger brother of John Perez Fabregues, count of Jaffa and Karpass, who died at the end of October 1473. Among the leaders were the Chamberlain Rizzo di Marino, James Zaplana, the head of the Secrete, the count of Roucha, Peter Davila, John Tafur, count of Tripoli, and the Cypriote Tristan de Giblet. See George Hill, *A History of Cyprus* 3 (Cambridge: Cambridge University Press, 1948), 664 for the leaders of the Catalan party and 665–73, for a detailed discussion of the coup.

When the commander learned that two royal galleys had sailed for Cyprus without reporting to him, and not knowing the reason for their journey, he sent there two galleys under the Dalmatian captains Coriolano Cippico and Pietro Tolomerio. He ordered them to pay a visit to the queen, greet her in his name and assure her that if need be, at her request the commander would arrive with the entire fleet. He also commanded them to come back with all speed if there were something afoot in the kingdom. In the meantime the duke of Crete, prompted by rumors, wrote to the commander that the Cypriotes were not sincere and were plotting a coup. Hearing this, the commander dispatched Vettor Soranzo, the legate of the fleet, with eight galleys besides the two that had already been sent to Cyprus to make sure nothing occurred detrimental to the kingdom. Without delay, Vettor sailed out of Modon and caught up with the galleys that had been sent earlier at Crete. He directed Coriolano to sail ahead and fulfill the commander's order, while he would follow up behind him with the rest of the galleys.

Meanwhile the archbishop landed in Cyprus, gathered his friends and compatriots, and persuaded them to seize the kingdom, assuring them that it would be easy to take it over by force. He explained that the son of King Ferdinand who wanted to marry the daughter of the king was still a child and she was a girl. He pointed out that their king was an infant, and where there were two children they would easily become masters if they could remove Andrea Cornaro, the uncle of the queen. The archbishop fabricated tales to allay their fear of the power of Venice. And these perfidious men, forgetting the oaths to serve the queen that they had most solemnly sworn on their faith, acquiesced to the malicious counsel of the archbishop and condemned to death that most guiltless man Andrea Cornaro, and swore to take over the kingdom tyrannically.

Consequently, on the next night at the agreed signal they all sprang to arms.[2] They first fell on the queen's doctor and a certain citizen called Polinzapa, both loyal intimates of the queen — who out of fear had fled into her chambers — and killed them under her arms. They then went to find Andrea Cornaro.[3] The latter, who had heard of the death of the doctor, fled toward the castle but was locked out by the castellan and hid between the double walls of the fortress. A certain Epirote called Nicola, a man of vilest reputation, gave him up to the conspirators.[4] They came to the walls and called him out, promising him safety on their word. Then the henchmen of the conspirators murdered him along with the son of his sister, his nephew Marco Bembo, despoiled them of their clothes and discarded their naked corpses. A steward of Andrea's buried them in the church of San Domenico.

Now, according to an old treaty, the Venetians maintain a praetor in Cyprus who dispenses justice among the Venetians on the island.[5] The praetor at that time was Niccolo Pasqualigo. The conspirators went to him and told him that Andrea had been killed by his soldiers, whose wages he had withheld out

2. The revolt broke out on the night of November 13, 1473. Andrea Cornaro, brother of Marco Cornaro, engineered the marriage of his niece Caterina to James II and was singularly instrumental in the Venetian takeover of the island. Banished to Crete and then Cyprus in 1457 for conspiring to rig the elections for the executive committee of the Senate, he aided James II with loans and became his counselor. After the king's death, he was the staunchest pillar of the Venetian party on the island.

3. Paul Chappe, seneschal of Jerusalem and a long-time royal servant loyal to the queen, and Gabrielle Gentile, the queen's personal physician and confidante.

4. The information about the Epirote is not corroborated by other Venetian sources, see Hill, *History of Cyprus*, 3:673–74.

5. Cippico uses the Roman designation for high judicial officer, *praetor*, for Venetian officials called *provveditore* and *bailo* in the vernacular.

of greed. Their affirmed they would maintain their loyalty to the queen and their friendship with Venice and asked the praetor to write to the senate of Venice and to the commander about how Andrea had been murdered, by his own fault, by his mercenary soldiers whom he had defrauded of their wages. The praetor knew right away that they were lying but to gain time promised them to do everything.

After that the conspirators went to the royal palace. There they betrothed the daughter of the king, a six-year-old girl, to King Ferdinand's son of the same age, promised him a large dowry and bestowed upon him the title of Prince of Galilee (among the Cypriots this title is given to the heir to the throne). This done, they sent the royal envoy that had come with the archbishop on one of the royal galleys to inform King Ferdinand of what had happened.

After that, fearing that the power of Venice would overcome them before they had entrenched themselves, they sent envoys to Venice and to the commander of the fleet to mitigate the outrage of Cornaro's murder and delay any possible military action against them. They sent letters written in the name of the queen and signed by her own hand to the commander and Senate contending that Andrea had been killed by his soldiers because of his greed, that she and her son governed the kingdom freely and that they were all loyal and obedient to her.

Forced by the tyrants, the queen did what they wanted; she wrote not what she pleased but what the conspirators ordered her to. Then the tyrants installed as castellans men loyal to them and cognizant of their crimes. And because there was no money in the treasury, the tyrants melted down much of the royal silverware and minted coins to pay the wages of their supporters.

*

[1474]

WHILE THESE THINGS were taking place, the two galleys that the commander had sent arrived in Cyprus and cast anchor at the reefs outside of the port of Famagusta.[6] Coriolano and his colleague figured out what had happened but decided to pretend ignorance for a while. Nonetheless, to lift the spirits of the good men and deter the tyrants, they decided to find a suitable manner to inform the queen that the legate was arriving with eight galleys and that the commander himself was expected a few days later. And so he appeared before the queen and announced that he had been sent by the commander to advise her that the commander had sent the legate with ten galleys because he had heard that the sultan, the ruler of Egypt, had promised the kingdom to Carlotta, the sister of the king. He also said that the sultan would soon arrive with the entire fleet. He said this so that it would become known to everyone that the Venetian senate and the commander himself would defend the queen and the kingdom of Cyprus against anyone.

The news brought some relief to the queen and all good men, but when the tyrants heard that, they began to despair of their safety. Four days later the legate Soranzo arrived with the eight galleys and stationed them outside the port, not wishing to enter the city. Two of the conspirators were given safe conduct and came to the legate.[7] They accused Andrea of greed, attempted to prove their and their accomplices' innocence before the legate and promised to place themselves and everything that was theirs under the protection of the Venetian senate. The legate realized immediately that their words did not align with their deeds but decided to try to induce them to acknowledge their error.

6. On November 19 or 20, 1473.
7. One of them was the ringleader, the archbishop of Nicosia.

To that end he responded to the conspirators that the murder of Andrea had been a private wrongdoing rather than a state offense. He confirmed that if they were to remain loyal to their king, the senate of Venice would consider them friends, but for that words were not enough, deeds were needed. Therefore, if their promises were sincere, they should restore the castles and the revenues of the kingdom to the queen. They promised to do it if the others agreed. After spending several days trying to help settle the differences among the tyrants and realizing that nothing would come from it but words, he wrote to the Senate and the commander that the queen and the kingdom were heavily oppressed by the tyrants and that he had not been able to bring the tyrants to a reasonable position with words. Therefore, arms and a major war effort were needed to liberate the kingdom.

The commander had already learned that Triadano Gritti had been designated as his successor, a man with acute intellect and well-versed in public affairs but of ancient age (for he had completed his eighty-fourth year). Two legates had been designated with him: Alvise Bembo, who had been a legate the first two years, and Jacopo Marcello, a courageous man and an expert in naval warfare.[8] He was expecting the decree that the Senate had sent to recall him home when an envoy of the conspirators arrived and apprised him of his mission. The commander admonished him sternly and let him go. Then, reflecting on the importance of the matter, he decided that

---

8. Triadano Gritti was the grandfather of Doge Andrea Gritti. He was an ambassador to England, France and Spain, as well as to Pope Paul II and had served as *podestà* of Padua in 1453 and captain in 1465. His last service was the office of captain general referred to here, for he died in Cotor, the chief city of Venetian Albania, in 1474. Gritti was appointed on October 8, 1473, but did not leave Venice before March 19, 1474. See ASV, *Senato mar*, Reg. 9, c. 160v; and ASV, *Senato, Secreta*, 26, 74r.

there was no time to lose. He called the admiral of the fleet and ordered him to prepare and get the ships ready.

There were there, coincidentally, seven great galleys: four that were to sail to trade in Alexandria and three prepared to go to Syria for the same purpose. The commander held them all from proceeding. He sent those that were to go to Alexandria to Crete to inform the magistrate there about the state of the affairs in Cyprus. There are many mounted soldiers in Crete who serve for pay. The foremost of them, at the time when the Venetians settled the colony, received estates against the obligation to serve on horseback. And so the commander asked the duke of Crete to gather as many as possible of the horsemen and load them on the Alexandria galleys. Apart from this he ordered him to load all cargo boats he could find with provisions and put on them mercenary soldiers from the urban garrisons and Cretan archers. All these were to sail to Rhodes where they were to wait for him, for he had decided to gather all troops in Rhodes and from there sail for Cyprus. He sent the three Syrian galleys to Nauplion and wrote to the city prefect to put on them as many horsemen as they could carry and send them to him in Rhodes. He was to collect soldiers from the garrisons around the Peloponnese and put them on the ships too. Furthermore, he was to load on every ship ten additional horsemen. The two great galleys, which usually carried supplies for the fleet, were to be loaded with victuals and artillery suitable for urban siege and as many horsemen as they could carry. Then he was to announce in all cities and isles of Greece that any Venetian ship that put in there had to sail to Cyprus on the pain of capital punishment and confiscation of their goods.

After quickly arranging all this, the commander set sail for Rhodes with the troops. On the way there he received the letter from the legate Soranzo in which he informed the commander how Cyprus had been oppressed by the tyrants, of the tyrants' plans and of his interaction with them. Finding out how things stood from the legate's letter, the commander sped up toward Rhodes. While he tarried there for a few days (since the equipment he expected had not yet arrived from all places so that he could take off for Cyprus with a powerful host and overcome the enemy), a letter arrived from Soranzo from which he learned that the tyrants had been seized by fear and had fled, and that the situation in Cyprus was under control.[9] But the queen wrote that even though the leaders of the tyrants had fled for fear when they learned of the army and the huge amount of military equipment under the commander, many remained who had been accomplices of the tyrants in everything and who had said and done much against law and custom. She affirmed that there were many more besides the evildoers who, relying on their power, now stirred trouble, and that the entire kingdom was in grave danger. Because of all that, she strongly urged the commander not to desert her and her kingdom, which was under serious threat, but to hasten to arrive with all of his troops to root out tyranny and pacify the kingdom.

The commander read the letters of the queen and legate, carefully considered everything, and decided to proceed to Cyprus with the entire force: first to liberate the kingdom from the oppression of the tyrants, and second to demonstrate to everyone how swiftly the power of Venice could be deployed when necessary. Thus, he left Rhodes with the entire army, sailed

---

9. The leaders of the Catalan conspiracy fled Famagusta on New Year's Eve on a Neapolitan galley, evaded the pursuit of two of Soranzo's galleys, and made it to Rhodes. Mocenigo himself arrived at Rhodes on January 25, 1474, and demanded that they be handed over, but the grand master turned down the request. Mocenigo decided not to press the issue and sailed to Cyprus to secure the island, taking with him only one of the conspirators, Tristan de Giblet.

for Cyprus and in a few days arrived in Famagusta.[10] There the commander ordered everyone to don their arms. Then he staged a parade on Piazza San Niccolo, in the city center next to the royal palace, in the presence of the queen and all of the foremost Cypriots, and displayed his troops. The queen and the magnates were stupefied when they saw the huge military force, admiring the competence and diligence of our commander who had gathered together such an outstanding army in the middle of winter, on roaring and tempestuous seas that at times impeded navigation, from so many places and in such a short time. After the roll-call of the troops, the commander gave leave to the merchantmen and all other vessels that had come from different places at his request, except the war galleys of his squadron. He sent home the horsemen of all kinds and the soldiers recruited from the garrisons, and kept only the Cretan archers. Then he appointed Venetian prefects over garrisons of Cretan archers and installed them in the castles.

Thereafter, since the queen had apprehended and kept in custody many of the accomplices of the tyrants after they fled, the commander put them to torture, condemned to death the participants and the accomplices in the murders and sent the suspects, regardless of their rank, into exile. On pain of burning and drowning, he banned from the island many evildoers and rebels who had hidden themselves. After a proper inquiry, he rewarded with the property of the tyrants those who had, out of loyalty to the queen, strongly opposed them. And so the commander had arranged everything and pacified and secured the kingdom, when letters arrived from Niccolo Marcello, the doge of Venice, with a decree of the Senate that put him in charge of the island of Cyprus. The doge instructed the commander on many aspects of the expedition — on retaining the merchant galleys, on the Cretan and Epirote horsemen and on

10. Mocenigo arrived on February 2, 1474.

the garrison soldiers — all things that the commander, with his astuteness and diligence anticipating the directives of the doge and Senate, had already done. It is a marvel indeed that the commander had already put into effect everything that the Senate commanded him to do for the preservation of the kingdom after the death of the king. There was nothing left for him to do, therefore, but according to the decree of the Senate it was necessary to stay in Cyprus to await the arrival of his successor.

  Meanwhile the new legate Jacopo Marcello arrived, sent by the Senate to the Peloponnese with money to recruit horsemen. Learning of the commander's arrangements, he gave up the task and brought him the funds. The commander took them and sent Marcello with ten galleys to defend the islands in the Aegean. Several days passed in expectation of the arrival of his successor in Cyprus without any news. Finally, he received letters from his successor informing him that he was in Greece but would not come to Cyprus because the commander had been tasked with conducting the affairs of the kingdom as decreed by the Senate. Receiving the letters of his successor and considering the affairs of the kingdom in good order, everything being quiet and secured, the commander decided to return home, for it was already time. He ordered the legate Vettor Soranzo, whom the Senate had put in command of the ground forces of the expedition, to remain in Famagusta with ten galleys for the protection of the kingdom. He himself visited the queen and, addressing her courteously, told her that through the power of Venice and his effort the kingdom had been freed from tyrants and restored to her. In the name of the Senate and in his own name he promised even more in the future if need be. The queen praised the commander and thanked the Senate and him personally, calling him a father and savior of the kingdom. As a sign of a job well and properly done, she gave him a shield of exquisite workmanship and a gold-embroidered banner of vermilion silk with the royal insignia. To the legate she granted smaller banners. The commander wished her well, kissed the royal child whom the queen mother held in her hands, and took his leave.[11]

*

LEAVING THE LEGATE BEHIND, he departed from Cyprus with the rest of the fleet. The journey was arduous, for the winds were adverse (as it was already summer) and they had to take to the oars. He came first to Rhodes, then to Crete and then to Modon. There he learned that a large enemy host had put under siege the town of Scutari, which for many years had been under Venetian rule.[12] Scutari sits on a high mountain, steep and precipitous from all sides, and at places inaccessible, in that part of Illyria that was occupied by the Epirotes and is now called Albania. It is a fertile province, abounding in everything necessary for people to live. To the west of the town there is a lake measuring eighty thousand paces in circumference. It is named after the town and is called Lake Scutari. A river issues from it; its current bathes the foothills of the mountain on which the town is situated. The locals call the river Boyana.[13] In ancient times, as Pliny testifies, the river Drin used to flow to the east of the town, but now it has changed its riverbed and

11. According to Sabellico, the queen also granted Mocenigo a fief, see Hill, *History of Cyprus,* 3:696 n. 1.

12. Venice acquired Scutari in 1396 from George Balshich, the son of the Albanian potentate Balsha II who was hard pressed by the Ottomans, in exchange of 1,200 ducats in yearly pension. After the loss of the city to the Ottomans in 1476, it became the capital of the *sandjak* of Albania.

13. Boyana or Buna in Albanian, is a 41-km.-long river that originates in Lake Scutari, the largest lake in the Balkans, and is shared between Albania and Montenegro. For shallow-keeled vessels the river is navigable up to the lake.

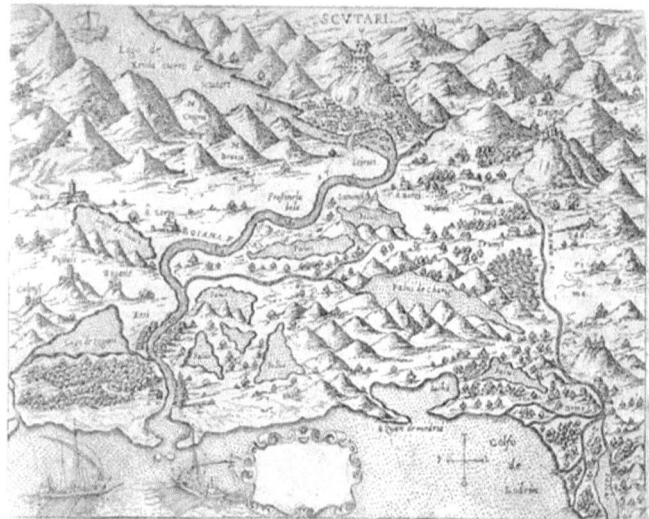

Fig. 16. Map of Scutari by Giovanni Francesco Camocio, c.1570.

flows close to Lesh.[14] It empties into the sea in two channels, ten thousand paces to the east of the estuary of Boyana. The dry bed of the river with vestiges of a bridge can still be seen at Scutari.

I wonder why neither Pliny nor Strabo, an extremely diligent geographer, make no mention at all of such an important lake and the river that flows from it. Both rivers are navigable and capable of supporting cargo ships many thousand paces upstream. The plain between them and the fields round about it

14. Drin (ancient Greek Δρινος) is the largest and most important river in Albania, total length of c.160 km. Lesh (ancient Lissos or Λισσός in Greek, medieval Alessio, modern Lezhë in Albania), was a Greek colony founded in 385 BCE by Dionysius I of Syracuse. In 211 BCE it was seized by the Hellenistic Macedonian kings and later became the capital of the Illyrian kingdom until the Roman conquest. After the disintegration of the Roman Empire the city remained Byzantine until the rise of local Albanian lords who bickered over it. Venice acquired it in 1386.

are so fertile that an accidentally dropped seed bears marvelous fruit without any hard work. It is said that the locals chase their sheep away from the grazing grounds lest they die from overeating. The region is surrounded by high and rough mountains. In the lower parts there are hills with intensely cultivated vineyards and olive groves. The coastal area, besides marshes, is covered by timber-rich forests that provide abundant material for shipbuilding.

For these reasons and because of the rivers, the Ottoman (who, it appears, hopes to occupy the entire world) considered this region most suitable for supporting armies, building ships and maintaining a fleet. He therefore decided to seize Scutari, the principal town and fortress of the entire province. (See Map 3.) If he conquered it, there was no doubt that the entire region would be his. He was hoping that after taking over Albania, on the example of the Epirote kings Alexander and Pyrrhus, the fleet could cross the gulf of the Adriatic with a large army and military apparatus and in this way conquer Italy, which they were unable to do due to insufficient resources.[15]

Therefore, he charged Suleiman, the pasha of Romania, with the task of seizing the town. Suleiman had been captured in Lower Pannonia, the province now called Bosnia, when he was still a child, and due to his beauty he was handed over as a

15. Alexander I of Epirus or Alexander Molossus (370–331 BCE), uncle of Alexander the Great, crossed the Adriatic in 334 BC to aid the southern Italian Greek colony of Taras and was killed in Lucania in 331 BCE. Pyrrhus or Pyrrhos (Greek Πύρρος) (319/318–272 BCE) was king of Epirus 288–84 and 273–72 BCE. In 280 BCE he crossed the Adriatic, landed in southern Apulia and led a five-year-long campaign against Rome, southern Italian powers, and Carthage. Cippico may have acquired his information from Livy or Plutarch, who wrote a *Life* of Pyrrhus. See Bernadotte Perin ed. and trans., *Plutarch's Lives in Eleven Volumes. 9 Demetrius and Anthony, Pyrrhus and Gaius Marius* (Cambridge, MA: Harvard University Press, 1920), 345–461.

gift to the Ottoman, who made him eunuch and used him in lewd ways.[16] Last year, as he was already of age, he was promoted to the highest magistracy in place of the pasha who fell in the Persian war. He was given about eight thousand Janissaries from the Ottoman's personal guard and a hundred men expert in the casting and operating of cannons. The pasha ordered all provincial governors on this side of the Hellespont who are under the Ottoman to join him with their troops and gathered five hundred camels to carry the copper for casting the cannons. When everything was ready, he marched the entire army to Albania, passing first through Macedonia and then through the province of the Tribals. His troops swarmed the area around Scutari. Here he made a roll-call and found out that there were eighty thousand men under him. Then he assigned everyone to their position so that the town was surrounded and ordered that it be carefully guarded so that no one could exit or enter. The gunsmiths began work on casting the cannons. The pasha ordered timber to be cut down from the nearby forest to build a bridge across the river on the seaside downstream from the town. Alibeg, a most brave Tribal commander, was posted there to guard the bridge with his troops.

When the commander learned of the siege of Scutari, even though he knew that his successor was on his way there with some galleys, he decided to depart immediately for Albania

16. There are several discussions of the role of eunuchs in the Ottoman Empire; see for orientation Baki Tezcan, *The Second Ottoman Empire: Political and Social Transformation in the Early Modern World* (Cambridge: Cambridge University Press, 2010), 101–5; Ahmed Akgündüz and Said Öztürk, *Ottoman History: Misperception and Truth* (Rotterdam: IUR Press, 2011), 403. The trope of the sultans's predilection of young pages and eunuchs is common in early modern descriptions of the Ottoman court. Mehmet II is specifically noted to have maintained over 200 boys in his harem to serve his sexual desires, see Pierre Hurteau, *Male Homosexualities and World Religions* (New York: Palgrave Macmillan, 2013), 149.

regardless, lest he fell short in his service to the Republic. At Corcyra he received letters from the doge of Venice and a decree of the Senate, which entrusted him with the defense of the province of Albania.[17] Accepting the charge of the Senate, without delay he set out for Albania with his legate Stefano Malipiero. At the entrance of the mouth of Boyana he joined with his successor Triadano Gritti and the latter's legate Alvise Bembo. According to the Senate's decree, Mocenigo could have captained the entire endeavor by himself, but because he was anything but ambitious and always placed the public good ahead of his pride, he decided to consider and carry out everything only after deliberating with his successor.

The Senate sent the legate Leonardo Boldu, a man skillful in the handling of many affairs who had lived many years in Albania, to take command of the ground forces of the expedition. The commanders sent him to Kotor with four galleys. Kotor is a town in Dalmatia, situated in the bay of Risan. It is a populous town and its territory is ample and densely settled. It was built by the Risonians who, vexed by long wars, left their original settlements and moved to a more secure site.[18] The

17. Corcyra, modern Corfu, ancient Greek Κέρκυρα, the second largest of the islands in the Ionian Sea. After a turbulent and contested history, Venice came to control the island in 1386, and in 1401 began direct rule, which it kept until the fall of the republic in 1797. It is known as "The Door of Venice" because of its location at the entrance of the Adriatic, and was massively fortified by Venice against Ottoman incursions, which began in 1431 and continued until the end of the Venetian domination.

18. Kotor, Italian Cattaro, town on the coast of the Gulf of Kotor in Montenegro, on the bay of Kotor or Boka Kotorska. Appearing for the first time in 168 BCE, the settlement was named Ascrivium by the Romans in their province of Dalmatia, and after the fall of Rome remained a mostly autonomous community during the Middle Ages. In the tenth century, when it belonged to Byzantium, Constantine Porphyrogenetus knew it as Decatera. It became part of

commanders ordered Leonardo to go to Ivan Chernoevic, the ruler of the Illyrians who live around the lake and is a friend and ally of the Venetians, to persuade the man to gather all troops, both his and those of the cities under Venetian sovereignty, and bring them overland to the aid of Scutari.[19] Leonardo himself was to construct boats to cross over the lake and go in succor of Scutari together with Ivan. After that they sent five galleys up the river Drin to guard Lesh, because Lesh is situated in a plain and is poorly protected.

In the vicinity of Lesh there is a large island, created by the river Drin as it enters the sea and divides into two channels. On this island denizens from almost all villages of Albania had found refuge with their possessions. For that reason, apart from the galleys, they sent many other well-armed vessels to defend the island. Durazzo too was secured with four galleys and a garrison of Epirote horsemen. This city became famous during the time of the [Roman] civil wars. Here Pompey gathered his military forces against Caesar. Nowadays because of the bad air it is deserted and largely uninhabited, but many magnificent monuments of the city are still extant, among them a copper equestrian statue standing next to the land-oriented city gate. It is not inscribed; some assert it is Theodosius, others

the Venetian domain in 1420 after Venice took over Dalmatia, and it remained Venetian until 1797. The bay of Risan derives its name from the Latinized form of the ancient Greek Ῥίζων, after the place-name Rhisinium, a city of the Illyrian tribe Rizuniti, modern-day Risano. It is mentioned by Cippico's main sources, Strabo, 7, 5, 7, and Pliny the Elder (Plinius III.22.147), and Ptolemy, II.17.12.

19. Ivan Chernoevic (1465–90), lord of Zeta (modern Montenegro). His allegiance to Venice went back to his youth, when he served as hostage to the duke of Hum, Stephan Kosača, and only Venetian intervention secured his freedom. Early in his reign he fell out with Venice, but soon changed course and in 1466 allied with it against the Ottomans and proved a staunch and faithful ally, most notably in the defense of Scutari.

Constantine. Since its harbor is very convenient, the Venetians protect the city with a garrison. They also sent troops and vessels to garrison Budua, Antivari, and Ulcinj. Ulcinj used to be called Colchinium, built by the Colchis. Its inhabitants still retain, I don't know how, some of the savage traits of their ancestors and are rough and inhospitable toward strangers.[20] The commanders positioned the remainder of the fleet at the church of St. Serge the Martyr, in view of the defenders. The church is fourteen thousand paces away from the sea, and there are five thousand paces from the church to Scutari. Upstream from the church the river is too shallow for the galleys and other large craft to pass. From that position, the commanders and the defenders exchanged fire signals every morning and evening to show their persistence. Eight thousand paces downstream from the church, rocky hills on both banks channel the Boyana River into narrow rapids. The locals call the site Scala.[21] A fugitive informed the commanders that the enemy was preparing beams and chains to close the course of the river. For that reason, the commanders directed the galleys to take over the site, and so did the enemy.

When our forces arrived, both banks were already teeming with enemies. The enemy pestered our troops with arrows; our men shot at the enemy with stones and lead balls from the guns and rounds of both kinds wounded many. And because our men were armored and protected while the enemy fought

20. Ulcinj, Roman *Olcinium*, an Illyrian settlement, is connected to the Colchis already in the third century BCE, by the Greek poet Apollonius of Rhodes in his *Argonautica*, and the tradition is present throughout the Hellenistic and Roman periods. Livy mentions the connection in 45.26. The tale about the Ulcinjans' attitude to foreigners dates from the Roman period. It was captured by Venice in 1405 and named Dulcigno, but Cippico eschews the Italianate name. Venice held the town until 1571, when it was conquered by the Ottomans along with the rest of Albania.

21. Meaning "The Rock."

exposed to their blows, not a single shot fired in the thickness of the enemy missed, and many of them were killed. And so, with many of the enemy killed and even more wounded, they turned their backs and left the place to our men. About five hundred Turks were killed in that battle. Even though many of our men were wounded by arrows, not a single one was killed. The commanders left four galleys to guard the site and returned with the rest of the fleet to the church of the martyr. In the meantime the pasha had cast four large cannon for demolishing walls and twelve smaller ones for the destruction of houses within the city. Day and night the guns assaulted the walls with frequent shots. These walls were not strongly built, were worn out and had deteriorated with time, so they easily fell apart.

Inside the fortress of Scutari was the praetor and legate of the whole of Albania, Antonio Loredan, the scion of a most noble family, a most courageous and indefatigable man, prepared to go through anything for the fatherland.[22] With great

---

22. Antonio Loredan (1420–82), of Sta. Maria Formosa, scion of a family of illustrious naval commanders, embarked on a career in the Venetian navy in his early twenties and had a long history of fighting the Ottomans. He commanded a galley at the age of 23 and in 1444 provided naval support to the crusade of Varna. After a brief interlude during which he married and served in several minor magistracies in Venice, he returned to the sea in 1460 as commander of a small armada sent to reinforce the Venetian outposts in the Morea. In 1466 he was appointed *provveditore* of the Morea. Between 1467 and 1471 he served as a count in Dalmatia. He was sent to Scutari in September 1473 as captain and *provveditore* for Albania. There he demonstrated extraordinary leadership throughout the siege, which lasted from July 15 to August 28, 1474. In September after Gritti passed away and Mocenigo became doge, Loredan was elected captain of the sea. Over the next several years he crisscrossed the eastern Mediterranean, visited Cyprus several times to strengthen the reign of Caterina Cornaro, attacked Ottoman outposts in Anatolia and conducted negotiations with the Sublime Porte. After the peace of 1479 he was elected procurator of

presence of the mind he kept an eye on everything and wherever he saw the walls failing, he ordered posts to be driven in the ground and fortified with horizontal beams. Then baskets filled with earth and horse manure, of which there was plenty in the town, were poured inside, and thus a bulwark was constructed, fifteen feet wide and twenty feet high. On top of the bulwark he positioned wine casks filled with earth in the place of battlements, so that the defenders could fight the enemy protected.

With great promises, Loredan convinced a dauntless youngster, Epirote by origin, to carry a letter of his to the commanders. The young man took the letter and on a dark and terrifying night, in the midst of a thunderstorm and torrential rain, rushed through the enemy camp and delivered the letter to the commanders. Antonio wrote in it that in terms of location, courage of the defenders and the defenses he had prepared, he deemed the position impregnable. However, since the outcome of the war was uncertain, he asked the commanders to hasten to bring him succor, although he recognized that that would be difficult, given that the enemy had placed strong roadblocks at all approaches to the city. The commanders read the letter and wrote to Leonardo to speed up the arrangements with Ivan. Leonardo had diligently organized everything, and Ivan had gathered a rather large infantry force, which he placed under the command of his brother George. Besides the four galleys that Leonardo had constructed, he had in his fleet thirty well-provided and armed river boats.

San Marco de Supra and toured Friuli as military inspector. In March 1482, at the beginning of the war of Ferrara, Loredan was appointed *provveditore* of the field army and took part in the early encounters but in the summer contracted fever and died in August 1482. See Giuseppe Gullino, "Loredan, Antonio," *Dizionario Biografico degli Italiani* 65 (Rome: Istituto della Enciclopedia Italiana, 2005), entry online at http://www.treccani.it/enciclopedia/antonio-loredan_(Dizionario-Biografico).

Fig. 17. View of the Fortress of Scutari by Edward Lear. From Journal of Travels through Roumeli during an Eventful Period. *London: Henry Colbourn, 1838.*

There is a mountain there, which extends like a promontory from the bay of Risan to the Boyana River. It becomes lower as it reaches the banks of the Boyana and levels up at Scutari. It is rough and rocky and impossible to pass by cavalry. Therefore on the appointed day George led the troops along the mountaintop to Scutari, while Leonardo set out with the fleet across the lake. The confraternities, which the Venetians call *scuole*, had provided seventy armed fishermen's boats because the galleys, due to the shallow river bed, were not able to navigate up to the fortress. The commanders sent the admiral with the squadron of these small boats to try to join up with our men. He had the boats covered from all sides with boards so that they were invulnerable to the arrows shot by the enemy from both banks of the river. Taking to the oars, they moved up against the current toward the city. The enemy, in the meantime, was not idling, for runaways had informed them of what was happening on our side. They placed twelve thousand picked horsemen under the command of Hamsa Beg at the foothills of the ridge from which George was expected to come down and doubled the garrison of the bridge. Upstream from the city, on the riverbanks where they feared Leonardo's fleet would arrive, they positioned several small guns and fortified the place with archers and other soldiers who were to fight back our men by shooting at them.

And so when George came down from the mountain, Hamsa Beg went against him with his troops arranged in battle order. As they came to a stone's throw from each other, they engaged from afar with arrows and other throwing weapons. The Illyrians, especially, who had the higher ground, picked off Turks by slinging rocks. George, due to the large number of enemy horsemen, did not think he would succeed in descending the mountain and entering the plain, while Hamsa Beg's cavalry, prevented by the broken, rough rocks, could not ascend the hill. When Leonardo attempted to move the fleet from the lake into the river, he found it dotted with fishermen's stakes as if deliberately posted to prevent the entry of a fleet. The fact is that in that place large quantities of fish are caught, from which the Venetians used to exact five thousand ducats in taxes.

Because our sailors were not able to proceed any farther, they engaged the Turks in hand-to-hand combat right away. Here a certain Turk rode around shouting impudently that if there were a Venetian brave enough to fight him in single combat he should come out of the board-clad boats. Then one of the allies in the army, Illyrian by nationality, sallied forth from the boat and leapt on the enemy. As the Turk tried to strike him with the scimitar, the Illyrian took the hit on his shield and then ran him through the side with his Norican sword, brought him down from the horse, despoiled him, cut off his head and took it to the boat where he threw it in the feet of the commander to great acclaim.[23]

23. Noricum was a Roman province encompassing the Styrian and Carinthian provinces of modern Austria and part of Slovenia. The area

Meanwhile the admiral with his squadron came to the bridge but, as he was not able to either pass or destroy the bridge because the enemy protected it, only shot at the Turks who guarded it with arrows and gunshots from afar. When our leaders figured out that they were trying in vain, however, they gave the signal for retreat, abandoned the endeavor and returned the men to their positions. Then they reported to the commanders that the pasha had fortified all positions with very strong units and argued that without a large cavalry force it would be impossible to bring succor to the defenders as the entire region round about was a plain. The commanders gave up expectation of relieving the town for the moment until the Senate provided them with a stronger military force and placed their hopes in the location of the town and the courage of its defenders.

In the meantime the new commander and his legate Alvise Bembo contracted a deadly disease. The whole area around Boyana is unhealthy and pestiferous, for its marshes and stagnant waters exude dense vapors and corrupt the air.[24] Pestilence badly afflicted and brought down the entire fleet. Therefore

---

is rich in iron deposits from which Roman iron and steel arms were manufactured. Horace has a reference to the Norican swords in his *Odes*, I.16.9–10.

24. "Corruption of the air" as a principal source of disease in marshy areas and places where putrid waste accumulated (rather than infection by malaria-bearing mosquitos) is a long-standing trope in Western medical lore. It was embraced by contemporary Venetian medical authors and authorities alike. See the documentary collection by Ivona Cacciavillani, *La Mal'aria: Ecologia ambientale nell'ordinamento della Serenissima* (Venice: Corbo e Fiore, 2008). The earliest recorded humanist discussion is by Cippico's contemporary Marco Cornaro, in the 1440s, see Giuseppe Pavanello, ed., *Marco Cornaro: Scritture della laguna* (Venice: Ferrari, 1919). On conceptualizing disease in the period see Mirko Grmek, "The Concept of Disease," in *Western Medical Thought from Antiquity to the Middle Ages*, Mirko Grmek, ed. (Cambridge, MA: Harvard University Press, 1998), 241–58.

Triadano and his legate Bembo departed for Kotor for the benefit of healthy air. Mocenigo, himself not very well, decided to wait out the end of the siege together with Malipiero.

The pasha had already razed to the ground the walls of Scutari, but Loredan had erected new ramparts made of earth and manure, which the artillery shots could not destroy since the material of the mounds absorbed the stone rounds of the cannon without any damage. A eunuch was sent to Loredan to demand the ruined and wrecked town. Were he to do that, he was promised great rewards by his prince and a foremost position with the Ottoman in the future; he better not wait till the town was taken by force for then the victors would do as they pleased with anyone, regardless of sex and social position. To this Loredan responded that he had been elected to defend the town not because he came from the scum of the Ottoman but because he stemmed from Venetian noblemen whose ancestors were not used to yielding towns to the enemy but to conquering cities and accepting the surrender of the enemy.[25] He treasured his faith, integrity and love of country far above any wealth or possession the Ottoman could give him. And if the pasha was a man and not a woman (as it was said) he would have quickly taken the town, stripped of its defenses.

At this the pasha, having lost any hope that Loredan would surrender, prepared wickerwork and protective sheds to cover his men as they approached the fortifications and ordered them to outfit themselves with grappling irons, hooks and sickles affixed on long posts. Ladders were not needed; the walls were demolished and they could climb on top of the ramparts. He also ordered that the first to climb were to carry

---

25. Both his father and grandfather had served as Venetian supreme naval commanders, captains of the sea. Pietro Loredan was the Venetian commander who accomplished to acquisition of Dalmatia and upper Albania in 1420.

the wickerwork and the sheds to protect those who came after them. Then the pike holders were to follow, among whom he placed Janissaries lightly armed with swords and shields only for easier scrambling up the fortifications. Behind them he positioned a large number of archers and other soldiers who were to harass the defenders with gunshots and other throwing missiles. Thus putting the army in battle order and appointing its tasks, before dawn he surrounded the mountain from all sides with countless troops and crept up to the town.

Meanwhile the defenders made ready to beat back the enemy. There were in the town many willow-woven baskets smeared with ox manure in which the inhabitants used to keep grain. They filled those baskets with tar, branches of forest pine, tow and sulfur that, set on fire, they were to throw upon the enemy. Huge rocks were prepared on the ramparts, and the large guns were stocked with smaller stones so that a single shot would hit many men. Thus prepared and bristling with throwing weapons, the defenders deliberately kept silent and waited for the enemy to appear under the fortifications. The Turks hollered a loud cry and rushed from all sides through the ruined walls to clamber on the ramparts. Now the defenders courageously began to pick off the enemy with their weapons and seized the grappling irons and hooks from many. They threw the burning willow baskets at the enemy, which turned into deathtraps that the Turks could not escape (because the slopes were thick with enemies), for the round baskets rolled down the inclines from above and burned down everyone on their way. Then the defenders hurled down rocks of enormous size, which often fell on the stones below and, as they picked up massive momentum with the rebound, smashed and destroyed throngs of Turks. Similarly, the grape shot of stones fired from the guns killed not only one but many of the enemy.

Undaunted, the Turks clambered up the piles of cadavers like beasts and pressed to reach the rampart, but the defenders covered all positions and with great courage and audacity rained down on them rocks, fire and missiles, decimating the enemy and pushing them back from the ramparts. Loredan was everywhere: he walked all around the place, monitored everything, and wherever he saw that the defenders were fewer, or wounded or tired, he replaced them with more and sound ones. He constantly exhorted and swore everyone in the name of the one true and immortal Christian God, in the name of the complete loyalty that they had given the Venetian senate (from which they stood to receive great rewards if they defended the city) to remember their virtue and Christian faith and to protect their country, wives and children from the cruel barbarian. The pasha too kept going around with his officers, clobbering the Turks with an iron mace to herd them to battle like cattle. The Turks began the attack two hours before dawn and continued till the fourth hour of the day without making any progress, falling dead on all sides and covering the corpses with new cadavers; finally, tired out and routed, they turned they backs and fled. The defenders sallied out and gave them the chase and pursued them, cutting them to pieces all the way to the foothills of the mountain. Then, after seizing many of their military insignias and overburdened with spoils from the dead, they returned to the city. In this battle the Turks lost three thousand men, among them fourteen high-ranking officers. A great number were wounded and the better part of them died later. Of the defenders only seven were killed, and fifty-nine were wounded. The following day the defenders heaped wood, branches and other combustible material on the bodies of the slain enemy and burned them down lest the fetid corpses pollute the air and afflict the inhabitants with a deadly disease.

When the commander learned how our men in Scutari did everything well and with success and no longer feared that the city would be taken, he decided to take proper care of his own health. For he grew sicker by the day, and he had heard that the legate Alvise Bembo had passed away in Kotor, that Triadano Gritti, his successor, was gravely ill and on the verge of dying and that many of the galley captains had paid their dues to nature. Fearing that the same was in store for him, he set out for Ragusa to seek medical attention, leaving behind the legate Stefano Malipiero. The latter was not well himself but promised the commander not to leave the river Boyana even at the prospect of certain death, before he had heard that the enemy had abandoned the siege of Scutari.

Ragusa is a city in Dalmatia that the Epidaurians constructed on a more auspicious site after the Goths destroyed their city of Epidaurus. It is a free city that has excellent laws and customs. It has a senate and magistracies and separate classes of patricians and commoners. Governance is solely in the hands of the patricians, and the commoners take care of their own business and are not interested in public affairs. This city surpasses all other cities in Dalmatia with its magnificent public and private edifices. It has an arsenal, and its port is closed by a chain. Its citizens are engaged in trade in many lands and are the richest of all Dalmatian towns. Here the commander consulted doctors and took potions and medicines to recover his health. The citizens jostled with one another to show him such courtesies as if he were a god who had descended from heaven to defend the Christian faith, for the fame of Commander Mocenigo's deeds had spread everywhere.

The pasha realized that he would not be able to seize Scutari by force and did not dare hold the city under siege any longer because he had heard that the Venetians had prepared a large force against him. He therefore ordered that the artillery he had cast be broken to pieces so that the copper could be carried away on camelback. Six thousand paces from Scutari there was a small fortress called Dagno, which was poorly fortified and which our men burned down and abandoned when the Turks came. The pasha, who wanted to show that he had accomplished something, ordered its walls razed to the ground. This done, he lifted the siege, dismissed his troops and returned to Macedonia. During the siege, the inhabitants suffered terribly from thirst, and this scarcity of water was their greatest affliction. From the non-combatants more than two thousand children, women and elderly people died of thirst, yet not a single defender thought of surrendering even as they saw their wives and children die in front of their eyes. If the siege had not been lifted — given that in the city there was water remaining for no more than three days and this only if everyone got only the smallest of rations — they had decided to sally forth armed, fall on the enemy and die fighting like men, avenging themselves with their blood. For that reason, as the siege was lifted, everyone ran to the river to drink the water for which they had thirsted so long. Many of them drank too much water and, overcome with dizziness and stiffness of limb, immediately fell down dead. The commander heard of the enemy's departure, and finding no relief from the Ragusan doctors and medicine, returned to Venice gravely ill. A few days later the new commander Triadano Gritti passed away in Kotor. Since with the departure of the enemy everything was now secure, Mocenigo's legate Stefano Malipiero dismissed the fleet. He ordered the galley captains to sail to more salubrious places and to attend to their and their crews' health, for due to Boyana's unhealthiness almost all of them were sick. Unwell himself, he set out for Venice.

*

✻ THE DEEDS OF COMMANDER PIETRO MOCENIGO

AFTER READING AND HEARING much about famous deeds of the Venetians, it is fitting to note at the end of this small composition that there is no commander whom I could have compared to Mocenigo, a commander with invincible courage. For who foresaw the future more wisely than he? Who arranged present affairs more prudently? Who administered everything with greater diligence and industry than he? Above all, anticipating all the intentions of the enemy, he never gave enemies a chance to harm him. He began and finished battles with equal audacity and cheerfulness. He endured fatigue, needed little sleep and ate and drank the soldier's fare rather than the commander's. Always thoughtful and intent never to give the enemy an opportunity to succeed, he never ceased to inflict grave damage to the enemy himself. Thus, besides seizing cities and devastating and despoiling provinces, he captured many Turkish merchantmen laden with goods and more than forty pirate's biremes with their skiffs. All captured pirates he strung up; their ships he either burned down or handed over to cities under Venetian rule. Because of that, for the four years he was commander, the Venetian republic did not suffer the least harm. I would place this man higher not only than our commanders but also than the most courageous and distinguished Romans. Quite unlike those full of vain ambition who craved the honors of this world and did everything for their own power, he was inspired always by true love for the Christian religion and his country and placed the public honor and good above all.

Honors he had enough; the more he avoided them, the more they accrued to him. For before he became commander he was a censor[26] and administered this magistracy with great dignity.

26. One of the two magistrates elected annually by the Great Council whose task it was to monitor the elections to the Great Council and the Senate, see Robert Finley, *Politics in Renaissance Venice* (New Brunswick, NJ: Rutgers University Press, 1980), 210–15.

Oftentimes in the Senate he had been the first one to be asked for his opinion, and he served many times as ambassador to the pope and the Roman emperor. While away as commander, he was unanimously elected procurator of San Marco by the Council, the first office in Venice after that of the doge. When he returned home not yet fully recovered, Doge Niccolo Marcello passed away, and he was installed as doge of Venice, the entire city concurring with the election. This dignity the Venetians consider to be equal to that of the Lacedaemonian kings. The doge is the prince of the Republic and the chief official of the city and governs with the approval of the Senate. In this only the Venetians differ from the Lacedaemonians: the latter elected their kings solely from two royal families, while the Venetians elect their doge from any patrician family that excels in customs and virtue.

And I pray to our omnipotent and immortal God that Mocenigo, who as commander bolstered the affairs of the Republic with his excellent and successful deeds, now as a prince and doge extends the auspicious Venetian dominion far and wide with his leadership.

*

THIS WORK WAS PRINTED in Venice by Bernard Pictor and Erhard Ratdolt of Augsburg together with Peter Löslein of Langenzenn, proofreader and friend. God be praised.

M.CCCC.LXXVII

* * *

Fig. 18. A Venetian Galley of the Fifteenth Century. From Bernhard von Breydenbach, Peregrinatio in terram sanctam. *Mainz: Erhard Reuwich, 1486.*

BIBLIOGRAPHY

EARLY MODERN EDITIONS OF THE LATIN TEXT
Cepio Coriolanus, *Petri Mocenici imperatoris gesta Venetiis*. Venice: Bernardus Pictor, 1477.

De Petri Mocenici imperatoris gestis libri tres. Item Conradi Wengeri De bello inter Sigismundum, archstrategum Austriae et Venetos libellus. Basel: Joannes Herold, 1544.

Chalcocondylas Laonicus, *De origine et rebus gestis Turcorum libri decem. Continet Coriolani Cepionis Petri Mocenici imperatoris Veneti gestorum contra Turcos libri III.* Basel: Ioannes Oporinus, 1556.

De bello Asiatico Coriolani Cippici Cepionis libri tres. Venice: Joannes Rampazzetto, 1594.

Pietro Giustiniani *Rerum Venetianum ab urbe condita ad annum 1575 historia... cui haec accesserunt opuscula... Coriolani Cepionis De Petri Mocenici Venetae classis imperatoris contra Ottomanum, Turcarum principem rebus gestis libri tres.* Strasbourg: Zetzner, 1611.

MODERN EDITIONS AND TRANSLATIONS
Fabri, Renata, ed. *Per la memorialistica Veneziana in latino del quattrocento: Filippo da Rimini, Francesco Contarini, Coriolano Cippico.* Padua: Antenore, 1988, 165–233.

Glico, Vedran, trans., *Koriolan Cipiko, O Azijskom ratu.* Split: Čakavski Sabor, 1977.

OTHER PRIMARY SOURCES
Barbaro, Giosafat. *Travels to Tana and Persia by Barbaro and Contarini: A Narrative of Italian Travels in Persia in the 15th and 16th Centuries.* London: Hakluyt Society, 1873. Facsimile ed., Cambridge: Cambridge University Press, 2009.

Cippico, Pietro. *Cronologia dell' Illustrissima casa Cippico dall' Anno 1171.* Trogir, 1708 (in manuscript).

Cornet, Enrico, ed. *Le guerre dei Veneti nell'Asia 1470–1474: Documenti cavati dall' archivio ai Frari in Venezia.* Vienna: Tendler, 1856.

Pliny the Elder. *Pliny's Natural History.* Harris Rakham et al., eds. and trans. Loeb Classical Library. Cambridge, MA: Harvard University Press, 1938–63.

Plutarch. *Plutarch's Lives* 3. Loeb Classical Library. Bernadotte Perrin, ed. and trans. London: Heinemann, 1914–26.

Sabellico, Marcantonio. *Historiae rerum venetarum ab urbe condita*. Venice: Torresani, 1487.

———. *Historiae rerum Venetarum. Degl' istorici delle cose Veneziane i qualli hanno scritto per pubblico decreto. Tomo primo, che comprende le istorie veneziane latinamente scritte da Marcantonio Coccio Sabellico*. Venice: Lovisa, 1718.

Strabo. *The Geography of Strabo*. 8 vols. Loeb Classical Library. Horace Leonard Jones, ed. and trans. London: Heinemann, 1917.

SECONDARY WORKS

Akgündüz, Ahmed, and Said Öztürk. *Ottoman History: Misperception and Truth*. Rotterdam: IUR Press, 2011.

Andreis, Paolo. *Storia della città di Traù*. Split: Hrvatska Stamparija Trumbic, 1909.

Babinger, Franz. *Mehmed the Conqueror and His Time*. William C. Hickman, ed., Ralph Mannheim, trans. Princeton, NJ: Princeton University Press, 1978.

Bakotich, Andrea. "Un carme consolatorio di Marcantonio Sabellico a Coriolano da Traù, (1492)." *Archivio storico per la Dalmazia* 12.69 (1931): 419–49.

Berić, D. "Cippico, Koriolan." *Leksikon pisaca Jugoslavije*. Belgrade: Novi Sad, 1972, 525.

Bombacci, Alessio. "Venezia e la impresa Turca di Otranto." *Rivista Storica Italiana* 66 (1954): 159–203.

Brown, Patricia Fortini. *Art and Life in Renaissance Venice*. New York: Prentice Hall, 1997.

———. *Venetian Narrative Painting in the Age of Carpaccio*. New Haven: Yale University Press, 1988.

———. *Venice and Antiquity: The Venetian Sense of the Past*. New Haven: Yale University Press, 1996.

Cacciavillani, Ivona. *La Mal'aria: Ecologia ambientale nell'ordinamento della Serenissima*. Venice: Corbo e Fiore, 2008.

Campolieti, Giuseppe. *Caterina Cornaro: Regina di Cipro, Signora di Asolo*. Milan: Camunia, 1987.

Carboni, Stefano. *Venice and the Islamic World, 828–1797.* New York: Metropolitan Museum of Art, 2007.

Cox, Eugene L. *The Green Count of Savoy: Amadeus VI and Transalpine Savoy in the Fourteenth Century.* Princeton, NJ: Princeton University Press, 1967.

Cronia, Alberto. *L'umanesimo nelle letterature slave: Corso di filologia slava dell'anno accademico 1947–48.* Bologna: Patron, 1948.

Delalle, Ivo. "Dalmatinski humanisti." *Novo doba* 8.1 (1925): 2.

—. *Trogir.* Trogir: Tourist Society of the Trogir Commune, 1969.

Di Ventura, G. "Niccolo Canal." *Dizionario biografico degli Italiani* (DBI) 17 (1974), entry online at http://www.treccani.it/enciclopedia/nicolo-canal_(Dizionario-Biografico).

Ferrari-Cupilli, G. *Cenni biografici di alcuni uomini illustri della Dalmazia.* Zadar: S. Artale, 1887.

Fincati, Luigi. "La perdita di Negroponte (luglio 1470)." *Archivio Veneto* n.s. 32 (1886): 267–307.

—. "L'armata di Venezia dal 1470 al 1474." *Rivista marittima* 19 (1886): 384–96; 20 (1887): 5–183.

Finley, Robert. *Politics in Renaissance Venice.* New Brunswick, NJ: Rutgers University Press, 1980.

Foscarini, Marco. *Catarino Zeno: Storia curiosa delle sue avventure in Persia, tratta da antico originale manuscritto, ed ora per la prima volta publicata.* Venice: Vincenzo Formaleoni, 1783.

Gavrilović, Zara. "Women in Serbian Politics, Diplomacy, and Art at the Beginning of Ottoman Rule." In *Byzantine Style, Religion, and Civilization: In Honor of Sir Steven Runciman.* Elizabeth Jeffreys, ed. Cambridge: Cambridge University Press, 2007, 72–90.

Gioffrè, Domenico. *Il mercato degli schiavi a Genova nel secolo XV.* Genoa: Fratelli Bozzi, 1971.

Gliubich, Simeone. *Dizionario biografico degli uomini illustri della Dalmazia.* Vienna: Leopold Sommer, 1856.

Goodwin, Godfrey. *The Janissaries.* London: Saqi Book Depot, 1997.

Gouffier, Choiseul. *Discors preliminaire du voyage pittoresque de la Grèce.* Paris: L'Impremerie de la Société Littéraire-typographique, 1783.

Grendler, Paul F. *Schooling in Renaissance Italy: Literacy and Learning, 1300–1600.* Baltimore: Johns Hopkins University Press, 1989.

———. *The Universities of the Italian Renaissance*. Baltimore: Johns Hopkins University Press, 2002.

Grmek, Mirko. "The Concept of Disease." *Western Medical Thought from Antiquity to the Middle Ages*. Mirko Grmek, ed. Cambridge, MA: Harvard University Press, 1998, 241-58.

Guglielmotti, Alberto. *Storia della marina pontificia nel medio evo dal 728 al 1499*. Vol. 2. Rome: Tipografia Vaticana, 1886.

Gullino, Giuseppe. "Loredan, Antonio." *Dizionario Biografico degli Italiani* 65. Rome: Istituto della Enciclopedia Italiana, 2005, entry online at http://www.treccani.it/enciclopedia/antonio-loredan_(Dizionario-Biografico).

———. "Pietro Mocenigo." *Dizionario Biografico degli Italiani* 75. Rome: Istituto della Enciclopedia Italiana, 2011, entry online at http://www.treccani.it/enciclopedia/pietro-mocenigo_(Dizionario-Biografico).

———. "Morosini, Marcantonio." *Dizionario Biografico degli Italiani* 77 Rome: Istituto della Enciclopedia Italiana, 2012, online entry at http://www.treccani.it/enciclopedia/marcantonio-morosini_(Dizionario-Biografico).

Hankins, James. "Renaissance Crusaders: Humanist Crusade Literature in the Age of Mehmed II." *Dumbarton Oaks Papers* 49 (1995): 111–207.

Heers, Jacques. *Esclaves et domestiques au Moyen-Age dans le monde méditeranéen*. Paris: Fayard, 1996.

Hill, George. *A History of Cyprus* 3. Cambridge: Cambridge University Press, 1948.

Hunt, David, Iro Hunt, and Peter Edbury, eds. *Caterina Cornaro, Queen of Cyprus*. Nicosia: Trigraph, 1989.

Hurteau, Pierre. *Male Homosexualities and World Religions*. New York: Palgrave Macmillan, 2013.

Inalcik, Halil. "The Ottoman Turks and the Crusades, 1451–1522." In Kenneth M. Setton, gen. ed. Harry W. Hazard and Norman P. Zacour, eds. *A History of the Crusades* 6. *The Impact of the Crusades on Europe*. Madison: The University of Wisconsin Press, 1989, 311–53.

Karaman, D.F. "Castel Vecchio." *Bullettino di archeologia e storia dalmata* 20.3 (1897): 44–48.

———. "Coriolano Cippico di Traù." *Annuario Dalmatico* 1 (1884): 171–82.

Krstić, K. "Cippico, Koriolan." *Enciklopedija Jugoslavjje*. Zagreb: Leksikografskog Zavoda, 1956, 2:328.

Lučin, Bratislav. "Kodeks Petra Cipika iz 1436." *Živa antika / Antiquité vivante* 57.1–2 (2007): 65–85.

Lucio, Giovanni. *Memorie storiche di Tragurio ora detto Trau*. Venice: Stefano Curti, 1674.

Luttrell, Anthony. *The Hospitaller State on Rhodes and Its Western Provinces*. Aldershot: Ashgate, 1999.

—. *Studies on the Hospitallers after 1306: Rhodes and the West*. London: Variorum, 2007.

Malipiero, Domenico. *Annali veneti dall'anno 1457 al 1500*. Francesco Longo and Agostino Sagredo, eds. *Archivio storico italiano* 7 (1843): 5–586.

Manfroni, Cesare. "La campagna navale di Pietro Mocenigo." *Rivista marittima* 11.6 (1912): 70–77.

Maxwell, John Francis. *Slavery and the Catholic Church: The History of Catholic Teaching Concerning the Moral Legitimacy of the Institution of Slavery*. Chichester: Barry Rose, 1975.

Meserve, Margaret. *Empires of Islam in Renaissance Historical Thought*. Cambridge, MA: Harvard University Press, 2008.

Mueller, Reinhold. "Venezia e i primi schiavi neri." *Archivio Veneto* 5th ser. 148 (1979): 139–42.

Nicol, Donald M. *The Byzantine Lady: Ten Portraits 1250–1500*. Cambridge: Cambridge University Press, 1994.

Paschini, Pio. "La flotta di Callisto III." *Archivio della R. Società Romana di Storia Patria* 53–55 (1930–32): 177–254.

Pavanello, Giuseppe, ed. *Marco Cornaro: Scritture della laguna*. Venice: Ferrari, 1919.

Pavlovic Lucich, Stefan. *Memorie di cose dalmatiche*. Zadar: Demarchi-Rougier, 1864.

Pederin, Ivan. "Koriolan Cippico, njegov odnos sprema Mletačkoj vlasti i njegove veze s Ugarskom dvorom." *Zbornik Zavoda za povijesne znanosti Istraživačkog centra Jugoslavenske akademije znanosti i umjetnosti* 13 (1983): 191–96.

Perojević, M. *Postanak Kaštela*. Sarajevo: Hrvatsko Drustvo Napredak, 1934.

Popović, Mihailo. *Mara Branković: Eine Frau zwischen dem christlichen und dem islamischen Kulturkreis im 15. Jahrhundert*. Mainz: Rutzen, 2010.

Praga, Giuseppe. "Il codice marciano di Giorgio Begna e Pietro Cippico." *Archivio Storico per la Dalmazia* 13.77 (1932): 210–18.

—. "Organizzazione militare in Dalmazia nel quattrocento e la costruzione di Castel Cippico Vecchio di Traù." *Archivio storico per la Dalmazia* 20 (1935–36): 462–77.

—. "Poesie di Pascasio di Lezze, Tranquillo Andronico e Marino Statileo in onore di casa Cippico." *Archivio storico per la Dalmazia* 21–22 (1936): 283–90.

Preto, Paolo. *Venezia e i Turchi*. Florence: Sansoni, 1975; 2nd edition, Viella, 2013.

Riley-Smith, Jonathan. *Hospitallers: The History of the Order of St John*. London: Hambledon, 2003.

Sabolich, I. "La Dalmazia gueriera." *Archivio storico per la Dalmazia* 5.30 (1928): 290–95.

Scott, S.P., ed. and trans. *The Civil Law including The Twelve Tables, The Institutes of Gaius, The Rules of Ulpian, The Opinions of Paulus, The Enactments of Justinian, and the Constitution of Leo* 1–2. Union, NJ: The Lawbook Exchange, 2001.

Setton, Kenneth M. *The Papacy and the Levant, 1204–1571*. Vol. 2. *The Fifteenth Century*. Memoirs of the American Philosophical Society. Philadelphia: American Philosophical Society, 1978.

Špikić, Marko. "Razmjene spoznaja o antici u poslanicama hrvatskog humanizma 15. stoljeća." *Colloquia Maruliana* 18 (2009): 63–79.

Stornaiolo, C. *Codices Urbinate Latini* 2. Vatican City: Biblioteca Apostolica Vaticana, 1912.

Tamaro, Attilio. *La Vénétie Julienne el la Dalmatie* 3. Rome: Imprimerie du Sénat, 1919.

Tezcan, Baki. *The Second Ottoman Empire: Political and Social Transformation in the Early Modern World*. Cambridge: Cambridge University Press, 2010.

Tenenti, Alberto. "Le schiavi di Venezia alla fine de Cinquecento." *Rivista Storica Italiana* 67.1 (1955): 52–69.

Verlinden, Charles. *L'esclavage dans l'Europe médiévale* 2. Ghent: De Tempel, 1955.

—. "Venezia e il commercio degli schiavi provenienti dalle coste orientali del Mediterraneo." *Venezia e il Levante fino al secolo XV.* Vol. 1.2. Agostino Pertusi, ed. Florence: Olschki, 1973, 911–29.

Vuletin, Ivan and Damjan Pavlov. *Iz povijesti Kaštela.* Šibenik: Josip Ferrari, 1916.

Walsh, Richard J. *Charles the Bold and Italy (1467–1477): Politics and Personnel.* Liverpool: University of Liverpool Press, 2005.

Woods, John E. *The Aqqunyunlu: Clan, Confederation, Empire.* Salt Lake City: University of Utah Press, 1999.

Žic, N. "Mletačka incunabula trogirskog autora." *Napredak* 10.2 (1935): 16–17.

—. "Iz ratnih uspomena Koriolana Cippica." *Napredak* 10.3–4 (1935): 34–40.

✳

Fig. 19. Venetian Galley under Sail. Drawing by Raphael. Venice, Accademia.

INDEX

A

Abhasians 16
Adalia. *See* Attalia.
Adriatic Sea xiii, xiv, xvii, xix, xxix, 75, 77
Aegean (Greek) islands xxv, 7, 28, 30, 61; Sea xvi, xxiii, xxv, 3, 72
Aenos 4
Aeolia 13, 22
Ajas Beg, subashi 53
Alanya 40
Albania xvii, xxiii, 3, 68, 73, 74, 75, 76, 77, 78, 79, 80, 85
Alessio. *See* Lesh.
Alexander I Molossus, king of Epirus 75
Alexander the Great 40, 75
Alexandria 69
Alfonso V of Aragon 7
Alibeg, Tribal commander 76
Amadeus VI, of Savoy xxvi
Anatolia 39, 58; as barbarian xxx; cities xxvii; coast xxv, xxix; eastern 28; Ottoman conquest 3
Anaxagoras 33
Ancona, March of 58
Anguillara, counts of 57
Antalia, province of 56
Antalya 17, 23, 24, 56; gulf of 40
Antioch 57
Antivari 79
Antonio the Sicilian xxv, xxxi, xxxiii, 35–37
Aphrodisias 41
Apollo, god xxiv, 1
Apollonius of Rhodes 79
Apulia 75
Aq Qoyunlu emirate xxv
Archelaus Sisines, king 33, 45, 46
Archipelago. *See* Aegean islands.
Argolis 13
Armenia, Little (Cilician) 28, 60
Artemisia, queen of Halicarnassus 20
Ascoli 58
Ascrivium. *See* Kotor.
Attalia 23, 24
Attalus II Philadelphus, king of Pergamum 23
Attalus III Philopator 14
Attica 3
Aurelio, Marco 9
Austria 83
Azerbaijan 28

B

Balaban of Smyrna 32
Balearics 21
Balkans xxiii, xxvi, 73; Ottoman conquest of 3
Balsha II, of Albania 73
Bar 37
Barbanicola. *See* Antalya.
Barbaro, Giosafat 38
Basel xxxv, xxxvi
Beirut 5
beheading 15, 20, 29, 32, 33, 54, 83. *See also* prisoners and captives.
Bembo: Alvise 7, 9, 68, 77, 84, 87, 88; Marco 65

Bergama. *See* Paleocastro.
Bodrum 18, 20, 29
Boetia 3
Boka Kotorska. *See* Kotor.
Boldu, Leonardo 77, 78, 81, 82, 83
booty and spoils xvii, xviii, xxix, xxxi, xxxii, 13, 15, 19, 20, 22, 27, 52, 54, 63, 65, 83, 87, 90; division of 21, 29, 33. *See also* commodities; prisoners and captives.
Bosnia 3, 75; Bosnians xxxiv
Boyana River 73, 74, 77, 79, 82, 84, 88, 89
Bozhich, Peter 53
Brankovich, George, despot xvi, 8, 9, 73, 81, 82, 83; Mara 8, 9
Brescia xxi, 4, 57
Brown, Patricia Fortini xxx
Budua 37, 79
Bulgarians 16, 59
Buna. *See* Boyana River.
Burgundy, court xxi; duke of xvii
Byzantium 39, 60

C

Caesar, Julius xxvii, 78
Caicus River 14
Calycadnus River 48
Çanakkale. *See* Kale Sultanieh.
Canal, Niccolo xxiii, 3, 4, 5
Candia. *See* Crete.
Capello, Carlo xx
Cape Stilari 33
Cappadocia 28
Cappello, Francesco 8, 9
Capraria 21
captives. *See* prisoners and captives.

Carafa, Oliviero, cardinal xxx, 18
Caria 16, 18, 20, 22, 54
Carinthia 83
Carthage 75
Castel San Pietro 18, 29
Castro 14
Catalans xxxii
Catalonia 63
Cattaro. *See* Kotor.
Caucasians 16
Cega, Peregrina xiii
Çeşme 11
Chalcis 3, 4, 5, 6, 8, 35
Chalkokondilas, Laonicus, *History of the Turks* xxxvi
Chappe, Paul 65
Charlotte of Lusignan, queen of Cyprus xxxiii, 55, 63, 67
Chelidonia 24
Chernoevic, Ivan 77, 78, 81
Chios 11, 15, 61
Christian League xxiii
Cilicia 24, 28, 38, 40, 41, 51, 56, 57, 58, 60; Cilicians 42, 47. *See also* Armenia, Little.
Cilicia Trachaea 40, 51
Cippico, Alvise xix
Cippico, Coriolano xiii, xv, xxiv, xxvi, xxxvi, 43, 64; ancient models xxi; champion of Trogir interests xix; Christianity xxii; classical virtues xxii; classicism xxvi–xxviii, xxxi, xxxii; crusade themes xxii, xxvi, xxxi; Dalmatian loyalties xxxiv; death xviii; *Deeds of Commander Pietro*

INDEX

Mocenigo xiii, xvii, xix–xxxvii; humanism xiii, xiv, xvi, xvii, xxi, xxii, xxiv, xxxi, xxxii, xxxiii, xxxv, xxxvi; landed estates xvii; marriages xiv; Muslim-Christian conflict xxx; religion xxix, xxxi; style xxi, xxvii

Cippico, Giovanni xxxvi; Pietro xxii

Circassians 16

Ciriaco d'Ancona xiii

Clazomenae xxv, 33

Clusians xxxiii, 37

Cnidos (Cnidus). *See* Knidos.

Coccinio, Michele, *De bellis italicis* xxxvi

Cocco, Niccolo 8, 9

Cocino 12

Colchinium. *See* Ulcinj.

Colchis xxvii, 79

commodities: camel wool 11; carpets xxix, 11, 17, 20, 25; cloth and clothing xxix, 11, 38, 65; copper and copperware 32, 76, 78, 89; fruit xvii, 28, 29, 75; *giambelotti* 11; goat wool 11; gold and silver 32, 38; grain xvii, 86; iron 84 n. 23, 85, 86, 87; mohair 11 n. 14; sheep wool 11; silk 11, 38, 73; spices xxix, 25; steel arms 84; wine xvii, 81; woolens 11, 38

Constantine I, emperor 77, 79

Constantine Porphyrogenetus, emperor 77

Constantinople 3, 4, 8, 9, 39

Corcyra (Corfu) 9, 77

Cornaro: Andrea 60, 61, 64, 65, 66, 67, 68; Caterina xxxiii, 10, 51, 65, 80; Marco 51, 65, 84

Corsica 21

Corycus 40, 41, 43, 45, 49, 57

Cos 18, 29

Cotor 68

Cremona xxi

Crespo: Niccolo 28; Violante 28

Crete 4, 9, 64, 65, 69, 73; archers 71

Crimea 3

Croatians 23

Cyclades 61

Cyprus xvii, xxi, xxvii, xxviii, xxx, xxxiii, xxxiv, 38, 40, 51, 55, 57, 60, 61, 63–73, 80; king of 10; revolt of xxvi

Cyrene 45

D

Dafni 8

Dalmatia xxiv, 4, 37, 77, 78, 80, 85, 88; Slavs of xx

Dardanelles 34, 35, 39

Datsa peninsula 16

Davila, Peter 63

de Andreis, Nicoletta xvi, xviii, xx

Decatera. *See* Kotor.

Deeds of Commander Pietro Mocenigo See Cippico, Coriolano.

de Giblet, Tristan 63, 70

della Rovere, Francesco. *See* Sixtus IV, pope.

Delos, temple of Apollo 17

Demre. *See* Myra.

di Marino, Rizzo 63

Dionysius I, of Syracuse 74

103

disease 84, 87
Drin River 73, 74, 78
Dubrovnik xx
ducats 15 n. 21; 73 n. 12, 83
Dulcigno. *See* Ulcinj.

E

Egypt: sultan of 67; under Mamluks xxxii
Elaiusa Sebaste 46
Eleusia 45, 46
England 68
Epidaurians 88; Epidaurus 88
Epirotes 13, 73; Epirus 75
Euboea xxiii, 3, 4, 5, 7, 8
Euboean Gulf 3
Euripides 33

F

Fabbri, Renata xxxvi, xxxvii
Famagusta 55, 57, 61, 62, 67, 70, 72; church of San Domenico 65; Piazza San Niccolo 71
Federico, duke of Urbino xxxv
Ferdinand of Naples, king 7, 9, 22, 45, 63, 64, 66
Ferrara 81
Finike 24
Fiscum 54
Flaminia 38
Forum of Cornelius. *See* Imola.
Fosco, Palladio xvi
Fourth Crusade 3
France 4, 68
Frasina, Pietro 32
Friuli 81

G

Gaius Mucius Scaevola xxxiii, 37
Gallipoli xxv, xxxi, xxxiii, 35, 36
Gelidonia. *See* Chelidonia.
Genoa xxxii; and Cyprus 55; control of Chios 11
Gentile, Gabrielle 65
Giacomo III, duke of the Archipelago 30
Giustiniani, Pietro, *History of Venice* xxxvi
Gligo, Vedran xxxvi
Göksu River. *See* Calycadnus River.
Greece, islands 69
Greeks 3, 4, 13, 16, 24, 33; Greeks and the Romans 1
Gritti: Andrea, doge 68, 80; Triadano xxvi, 68, 77, 85, 88, 89
Guarini, Battista xvii
Guerra, Domenico and Giovanni Battista xxxvi

H

Halicarnassus xxv, 20, 21
Hamsa Beg 82, 83
Hasim Beg 48, 49, 50
Hellespont 35, 36, 54, 56, 58. *See also* Dardanelles.
Herceg Novi 37
Herodotus 45
Holy League xxx
Homer 33
Horace 84
Hospitallers xxxii, 10, 18, 45
Hum 78
Hungary, kingdom of xxiii
hunting 23

I

Illyria 73, 74; Illyrians 23, 26, 78, 83
Imola 38
Ionia 11, 30
Ionian Sea 77
Iran 28
Iraq 28
Isauria 40
Islam xxxiv, xxxv; mosques 31
Ismael, Janissary 47–49
Ivanishevich, George xvi, xx
Izmir. *See* Smyrna.

J

Jaffa 63
James II of Lusignan (Cyprus) xxvi
    10, 51, 55, 57, 63, 65
James III of Lusignan (Cyprus) 51, 60
Janissaries xxix, xxxiv, 46, 47, 48, 52,
    59, 76, 86
Jerusalem 65
Jezhevo 8
John II of Lusignan (Cyprus) 55
John of Portugal (Coimbra) 55
Justinian's Codex xviii

K

Kale. *See* Myra.
Kale Sultanieh 35
Karadja, Janissary 52–54
Karamanian lords xxv
Karamanids xxxii, 3, 39, 40, 41, 42,
    45, 48, 50, 51
Karpass 63
Kasim Beg 41, 42
Kilitbahir (Key of the Sea) 35
Knidos 16, 54
Knights Hospitaller. *See* Hospitallers.
Korghos (Korku). *See* Corycus.
Kosača, Stephan 78
Kotor 77, 85, 88, 89
Kurdistan 28

L

Lacedaemonians 91
Lake Scutari 73
Langenzenn 91
Lars Porsena xxxiii, 37
Lemnos 9–12
Lepanto, battle of xix
Lesbos 13
Lesh (Lezhë, Lissos) 74, 78
Livy 75, 79
Lodi, Giacobina xvi
Lombardo, Alvise 43
Loredan: Alvise 57–58; Antonio
    xxxi, xxxiii, 80, 81, 85; Pietro xiii,
    85, 87
Lorimo River 52
Löslein, Peter xxxv, 91
Louis I of Savoy 55
Lovrinac, Venetian vicar xx
Lucania 75
Lycia vi, 24, 41, 51, 52, 56
Lydia 54

M

Macedonia 8, 76, 89; Macedonian
    dynasty 74; Macedonians 59
Maina 18
Majorca 21
Malipiero: Domenico xxxvi;
    Marino 7, 9; Stefano 12, 24, 26,
    77, 85, 88, 89; Troilo xvii

Mamluks 55. *See also* Egypt.
Manutio, Aldo, the Younger xiv
Marcello: Jacopo 68, 72; Niccolo, doge 71, 91
Matthias Corvinus, king xvi
Mausoleum of Mausolus 20
Mediterranean xxii, xxiii, xxiv, xxviii, xxx, xxxii, xxxv, 80
Mehmet II (the Conqueror) xxv, xxviii, 1, 3, 4, 28; and Antonio the Sicilian 37; attack on Euboea 3; conquers Karamans 39; harem 76
Melo River 33
mercenaries 13, 39, 50, 66, 69
Mersin 39
Mestre 7
Mocenigo, Pietro xiii, xvi, xx, xxiii, xxiv, xxv, 1, 2; as leader xxxi; as model xxii; defense of Euboea 4; early life 5
Mocenigo, Tommaso 4, 5
Modon 11, 12, 18, 33, 34, 61, 64, 73
Montenegro 73, 77, 78
Morea xxv, 3, 80
Morelli, Jacopo xxxvi
Morosini, Marcantonio xvii, xx, xxi, xxvii, xxviii, 1
Mount Athos 8
Mount Taurus 24
Muhammad xxx, 13, 31
Murat II 3, 8
Muslims xx, xxii, xxx, xxxii, xxxiii, xxxiv, xxxv, 16 n. 22, 29 n.42, 46
Mustapha 42, 44, 45, 47, 49
Mycra 52

Myndi (Myndus) 29
Myra 52, 56
Myrina 12. *See also* Paleocastro.

N

Naples 7, 9, 18, 63
Nauplion 13, 34, 38, 69
Naxos 30
Negroponte xxiii, xxv, xxviii, 95; fall of xvi
Nicola of Epirus 65
Nicosia 51, 63, 67
Noricum 83

O

Octavian Augustus, emperor 46
Olcinium. *See* Ulcinj.
Oppidum Veneris. *See* Aphrodisias.
Orsini: Cencio 45; Giovanni Battista 10
Otlukbeli, battle of 60
Otranto xxviii, 94
Ottomans: attack Euboea 3; Balkans xxiii; empire xxviii, xxxiii; eunuchs 76; fleet 4, 11, 12; Levantine coasts xxiv; naval arsenal 35; Persian war 76; polity xxvii; Sublime Porte 80; *subashis* 32; sultan xxxi, xxxiii; territorial advances xxii; tyranny xxxiv

P

Padua xiv, 68, 93
Palaiologina, Elena, princess 55
Paleocastro 12
Pamphylia 23, 27
Pannonia, Lower 47, 75

INDEX

papacy xxx, xxxii, 9, 18, 24, 34, 57, 58, 61, 91; slavery 29
Papanicola. *See* Barbanicola.
Parisoto, Jacopo 14
Pasqualigo, Niccolo 65
Paul II, pope 68
Peace of Lodi 4
Peloponnese 7, 12, 13, 18, 27, 33, 61, 69, 72
Perez Fabregues: John 63; Louis 63
Pergamum xxv, 14, 23
Perotti, Niccolò xiv
Persia 28, 38, 39, 41, 42, 51, 56, 58, 60, 61; army 59; pestilence in 84
Philip of Burgundy, xxiii
Physcus. *See* Fiscum.
Piceno 58
Pico della Mirandola, Giovanni xiv
Pictor, Bernard xxxv, xxxvii, 91
Pindar 45
Pir Ahmed 39, 40, 41
Pliny the Elder, *Natural History* xxvii, 19, 73, 74, 78
Plutarch xxiv, 75; Julius Caesar xxvii
Polinzapa, Cypriot doctor 65
Pompey 78
Pontano, Giovanni xiv
Portogruaro 4
Portus Cavalerius. *See* Aphrodisias.
prisoners and captives xxv, xxix, xxxiii, 4 n. 3, 15–16, 18, 20, 21, 29 n. 42, 31–33, 46, 52, 54
Provençals xxxii
Psyra 30
Ptolemy 78

Pyrrhus (Pyrrhos) of Epirus 75

Q

Querini, Lazzaro 28

R

Radosich xvi
Rado the Dalmatian 36
Ragusa xxxi, 88
Rampazetti, Antonio xxxvi
Ratdolt, Erhardt xxxv, 91
Ravenna 7
Rechaiense (Requesnes) 7, 18
Rhisinium. *See* Risan.
Rhodes xxxii, 10, 18, 24, 28, 40, 54, 55, 57, 61, 69, 70, 73; Rhodians 25, 26
Rhodia Perae 54
Rimini 57
Risan (Risano) 77, 78, 82
Rizuniti 78
Romania, Turkish 58
Rome 37, 55; civil wars 78; conquest of Illyria 74; empire 14, 74, 77; Pyrrhic war 75; Romans 90
Roucha 63
Russians 16

S

Sabellico, Marco Antonio xvi, xviii, xxxvi, 37
Samos 22, 24
Satalia xxv, xxxi, xxxiii. *See also* Attalia.
Savoy xxi, xxvi, 55
Scutari xxvi, xxxi, xxxiii, 73–89; church of St. Serge the Martyr,

107

79; Dagno fortress 89; Scala 79
Seleucia 40, 41, 48, 49
Seleucus I Nikator 40, 48
Sequin. *See* Syedra.
Serbia 8, 59; Ottoman conquest 3; slaves 16
Seven Wonders of the World 20–21
siege warfare xxxi, xxxiii, 4, 23, 27, 37 n. 3, 49, 50, 53, 57, 69; Cilician campaigns 40–44; Scutari campaign 73, 76, 80 n. 22, 85, 88, 89
Sighun. *See* Syedra.
Sigismund, emperor xiii
Sixtus IV, pope 9
slavery xxix, 15, 26, 27, 29 30 n. 42, 35; Italian 16; papacy 29. *See also* prisoners and captives.
Slovenia 83
Smyrna xxv, xxix, xxxiv, 30, 31; antiquities 33
Soranzo, Vettor 12, 24, 25, 42, 50, 64, 67, 69, 70, 72
Spain 63, 68
Split 57
spoils. *See* booty and spoils.
Sporades 61
Sta. Maria Formosa 80
St. Panagia 15
Strabo, *Cultural Geography* xxvii, 74, 78
Strasbourg xxxvi
Strumitza 8
St. Theodore, port 40
Styria 83
Sublime Porte. *See* Ottomans.
Suleiman, pasha of Romania 75
Sultan's Fortress. *See* Kale Sultanieh.

Syedra 40
Syria 38, 48, 58, 69

T

Tabia 20
Tabriz 28
Tafur, John 63
Taras 75
Taşucu 48
Termerio 29
Termo 58
Theodore, envoy 9
Theodosius, emperor 78
Thrace 39, 59; Thracians 59
Tocat 28
Tolomerio, Pietro 64
Tommaso of Imola 38
Treviso 57
Tribals 52, 59, 76
Tripoli 63
Trogir (Trau) xiii, xiv, xv, xvi, xvii, xviii, xix, xx, xxii, xxiv, 43
Turcomans 28

U

Ulcinj xxvii, 79
Umbria 57
Urbino xxxv
Urla 33
Uzun Hasan, king of Persia xxiii, xxv, 28, 38, 39, 40, 56, 57, 60

V

Varna, crusade of 80
Venger, Conrad, *De bello inter Sigismundum Archistrategum Austriae et Venetos* xxxv

Venice 39, 42, 57, 61; Adriatic fleet 5; Aegean possessions 4; avogador di Comun 5; captain general of the sea xxiii, 4, 5; captain of the sea 12; colonial empire xix–xxxvi, 4, 64, 66, 68, 70, 71, 72, 73, 74, 77, 78, 79, 80, 89, 91; Council of Forty 7; Council of Ten 4, 5, 7; entrepôts and naval bases xxviii; foreign policy xxii; Great Council 90; as *La Serenissima* xix; legate of the fleet 7, 12, 16, 24; reprisals xxviii; San Marco 91; San Marco de Supra 81; scorched-earth tactics xxxiv; Secrete 63; Senate xvi, xvii, xviii, xxv, xxx, xxxi, 4, 9, 22, 28, 37, 51, 52, 56, 65, 66, 67, 68, 71, 72, 77, 84, 87, 88, 90, 91; slavery xxix; Small Council 7; terraferma xxviii, xxxiii; warfare xxviii; war with Ottomans, 1463–79 22
Venus, goddess 40
Verona 7

W

Wallachia 3
White Sheep Confederation 28
Wintner, Rudolf xxxv

Y

Yusuf, Karamanid prefect 45

Z

Zadar xiii, xviii
Zamperio (Juan Perez Fabriques, count of Carpass) 40
Zane, Lorenzo 57
Zaplana, James 63
Zeno: Catarino 28, 38, 56, 58, 60; Niccolo 28
Zeta (Montenegro) 78
Zetzen, Ludvig xxxvi

This Book Was Completed on September 30, 2014
At Italica Press in New York, NY. It Was
Set in Adobe Bembo and Bembo Expert.
This Print Edition Was Produced
On 60-lb White Paper
in the USA and
Worldwide

✻